A RETURN TO THE ORIGINAL JESUS

"The Christ of the Revelation is not the Christ of modern liberalism. He is the Christ whom we see in the Gospels, the Christ of Bethlehem's virgin birth, of Calvary's cross, and of the open sepulcher. He is the Christ who makes men dissatisfied with themselves as they are and with the world as it is, and who tells us that through Him life may be transformed and the world overcome."

THE REVELATION OF JESUS CHRIST—A popular understanding of the Revelation and its sublime and eternal values.

"Food for the soul. Deeply spiritual. A distinctive contribution to the study of the Book of Revelation. Good reading for the average Christian and trained theologians."—*Christian Observer*

"Clear, meaningful, conservative, understandable."—*Church Herald*

"Characterized by clarity of thought, excellence of diction and beauty of expression. Written by one who is universally esteemed and of unquestioned scholarship, sound judgment and gracious spirit."—*Union Seminary Review*

"Soundly written. One can spend more, but it would be difficult to find more value than in this paper-back reprint."—*Watchman-Examiner*

"A commentary in which eschatology, exhortation, and comfort are ideally blended."—*Theology Today*

"Worth reading. Would serve well as a leader's guide or student's resource book in lay group Bible study."—*Augsburg Book News*

"Help for every Christian."—*United Evangelical*

"Blessed is he that readeth, and they that hear the words of this prophecy, and keep those things which are written therein: for the time is at hand."—Revelation 1:3. (K.J.V.)

THE REVELATION OF JESUS CHRIST

DONALD W. RICHARDSON

JOHN KNOX PRESS   ATLANTA

Published by Pillar Books for John Knox Press

International Standard Book Number: 0-8042-3597-X

Library of Congress Catalog Card Number: 57-8522

© M.E. Bratcher 1964

First mass paperback edition 1976

Printed in the United States of America

PREFACE

The contents of this book were originally delivered as a series of five lectures. The informed reader of literature on the Apocalypse will find in them very little that is original. The author has no desire to win distinction through originality in speculation or in method of presentation. His sole purpose in publishing this material is to fulfill the request of many kind friends that the lectures be made available in printed form, and also to aid in the popular understanding of the Revelation and so increase the appreciation of its sublime and eternal values. For this reason the informal lecture style is retained and very little space is given to the discussion of purely critical questions concerning the composition of the book and the many conflicting theories of interpretation. John Calvin (who refrained from writing on the Revelation) in his exposition of Daniel 7:25 has a delightfully naïve statement: "Interpreters differ widely about these words, and I will not bring forward all their opinions, otherwise it would be necessary to refute them, but I will follow my own custom of shortly expressing the genuine sense of the prophet, and thus all difficulty will be removed." We follow the good example of Calvin! In doing so and thus avoiding all the subtleties of the controversial method, it should be possible within the brief compass of a few lectures to express simply and intelligibly the central teaching and present-day value of the book of Revelation.

The literature on the book of Revelation is very extensive, and much of it not of great value. Those who wish to make a careful firsthand study of the book will find that it cannot be understood without some knowledge of the Jewish Apocalyptic literature. The following works on Revelation will be found helpful: Alford, *The Greek Testament*; Charles, R. H., *A Critical and Exegetical Commentary on the Revelation of St. John*, and also *Studies in the Apocalypse*; Dean, J. T., *The Book of Revelation*, and also *Visions and Revelations*; Elliott, *Horae Apocalypticae*; Kuyper, *The Revelation of St. John*; Lenski, *The Interpretation of St. John's Revelation*; Milligan, *The Book of Revelation* (in the *Expositor's Bible* series); Morris, *The Drama of Christianity*; Ramsay, *The Letters to the Seven Churches of Asia*; Swete, *The Apocalypse of St. John*; Warfield, *Biblical Doctrines*, chapter XVI. Charles' *Studies in the Apocalypse*, mentioned above, has a good introductory chapter on the history of the interpretation of Revelation. Among the more recent helpful expositions of the book of Revelation are *The Meaning and Message of the Book of Revelation* by Edward A. McDowell (1951); *The Alpha and the Omega* by Paul Erb (1955); and *Explanation of the Book of Revelation* by C. H. Little (1950). The dispensational interpretation of the book in one of its simpler forms is clearly set forth in *The Holy Bible: Scofield Reference Edition*. This very limited list of books, representing different systems of interpretation, will provide a satisfactory background for further study and serve as an aid in formulating one's own convictions concerning the meaning and value of this very wonderful, very sublime, and at the same time very simple, book of Revelation.

SUPPLEMENTARY BIBLIOGRAPHY (1964)

Love, Julian Price, *1, 2, 3 John, Jude, Revelation* (Volume 25, *Layman's Bible Commentary*); Gettys, Joseph M., *How to Study the Revelation*; Barclay, William, *The Revelation of John* (two volumes, *Daily Bible Study Series*); Pieters, Albertus, *Studies in the Revelation of St. John*; Wernecke, Herbert H., *The Book of Revelation Speaks to Us*; Rowley, H. H., *The Relevance of Apocalyptic.*

CONTENTS

CHAPTER I

INTRODUCTION

1. *The Apocalyptic Method*

IN HIS *Keynote Studies in Keynote Books of the Bible*[1] Dr. C. A. Smith has an introductory lecture on "The Keynote Method" in which he says: "We have a right to ask of any work of literary art . . . , What does it mean? What truths does it embody and enforce? . . . A well-known literary critic has said that literature is that kind of writing in which the form is of more importance than the content. It would be hard to pack more vacuity into an equal number of words." Such a definition of literature is just as enlightening as is the definition of classical music as "music that is better than it sounds"; or the definition of a violin solo as the noise made by scraping the hairs of a horse's tail across the dried entrails of a dead cat. The book of Revelation has a peculiar form and literary method, but it has also a wonderful meaning, and the content of the book is of far greater importance than the form. The Revelation is a divine document and also a human document, and this one fact suggests many avenues of thought by which the student is constantly tempted to turn aside from the central current of the author's ideas.

As we approach our study of the book there are certain facts that we should constantly bear in mind:

1. The book of Revelation is not an easy book to interpret. There is a certain obscurity about the book. There was a reason, however, for its cryptic character; and whatever obscurity of meaning it may have for us

[1] Sprunt Lectures, 1917. Quotations used by permission of Fleming H. Revell Company, publishers.

today, it is not an obscurity due to ignorance or unclear thinking and writing on the part of the author. It was necessary for him to write in a way that would conceal his meaning from those outside of the Christian communion, and at the same time make his message clear to those for whom he wrote. The writer of the Apocalypse was an artist in the use of words and phrases and figures with a double meaning. For the safety of himself and those to whom he wrote he used symbols, mystical numbers, veiled references, and various other literary devices which would make his words entirely inoffensive to the ordinary and hostile Roman reader, and which at the same time would convey a deep spiritual meaning to those initiated into the Christian circle of ideas and expressions.

The fact that the Revelation is characterized by an intentionally symbolic and cryptic character adds to the difficulty of its interpretation. The author may make a direct reference to some contemporary event or person, the real meaning of which reference was known to his readers but which we shall never be able to fix with absolute certainty; but behind the specific reference there is the revelation of a general principle which has value for the reader in all lands and in all ages. Some readers of the Bible today frankly neglect the Revelation because of this seeming obscurity. Others read the book and their minds dwell upon the obscurities. Some people in studying the Bible have great facility in discovering only the passages difficult of interpretation. In the Old Testament they remember the imprecatory Psalms, Balaam's ass, Elisha's two she-bears, Jonah's whale; and in the New Testament the thing that impresses them most is the incident of the Gadarene swine. Their minds are always dwelling upon the difficulties. So also a great many people do not find the purpose and the power of the book of Revelation because they become fascinated with symbolic numbers and apocalyptic figures; and they make their minds linger and eddy around these minor obscurities instead of moving on with the great central current of divine rev-

13

elation. You can put two men down by the side of the sea. One is thrilled by the majestic sweep and surge of the waves. The other, "with never a vision within him to glorify his clay," would like to make a chemical analysis and determine the amount of salt present in the water. The book of Revelation, like Mrs. Browning's earth, is "crammed with heaven," but only those who see take off their shoes. The others "sit round and pluck blackberries." We should come to the book with the imaginative and inspired soul of the poet, and not with the exact and literal mind of the higher mathematician. A servile literalism will miss the book's purpose and magnificent meaning. In the Revelation we have the record of beautiful and high and inspired and holy thoughts. The book partakes of the character of poetry in its purest form; and you cannot read it as you read the Gospels, or the book of Acts, or any one of the New Testament Epistles. You cannot study Revelation as you would study a legal document or a chemical analysis or an algebraic formula.

2. Because of its symbolic and figurative character the book of Revelation is a much debated book. It has been made the basis for all sorts of fantastic schemes and systems of interpretation, and has been the happy hunting ground for the most fanciful theorists in the field of eschatology. I have before me the prospectus of a Bible school's correspondence course on "Revelation Revealed" in which it is stated that it requires one hundred and seventy-five keys to unlock the mysteries of the book of Revelation. "They are the one hundred and seventy-five symbols used by the angel in signifying the book of Revelation to John." There are eighty-one actors, according to this prospectus, in the Revelation Drama; and there are fourteen hundred and forty Thought Units advanced or suggested in the book. Those who enroll for this course and pay the required fees are supplied with a chart which will give "a mental picture of about what time in history any part of Revelation occurred, and what parts of Revelation are doubled and how many times doubled." The course

of study also emphasizes certain "startling things in Revelation," among which are the following: How the Church looks to dead people; The souls of the dead conversing and what they wear; Two hundred million flying machines described; When the Devil became a member of the Church; When and how the Devil was turned out of the Church; The Devil's son, grandson, and the whole Devil family. There is a list of thirty-five similarly striking and suggestive titles of subjects which are developed in this course of study. Not all the dispensational mishandling of the book of Revelation has been so eloquently ignorant as the sample here quoted; and yet the "lunatic fringe" of thinking on the times and seasons and last things of history has always revelled in the Revelation.

One reason why the last book in the Bible has been neglected by intelligent readers is probably the fact that it has been so pitifully mistreated by many of its so-called interpreters. We should approach the book with that humility of spirit which is willing at times to frankly say, "I do not know." There are passages in the Revelation about which no man can be dogmatic. We should not let our minds dwell upon those minor obscurities about which good and intelligent men and women always have differed and always may differ until they reach the glory world. We should be concerned about the message and the value of the book for our generation. We should let this word of God for the first century become for us the word of God for the twentieth century. We should read it contemporaneously, putting ourselves back in the age in which it was written; and we should read it individually, seeking the message for us today. John was a child of his age and spoke to the people of his age. He was also a prophet and apostle of the Church of the living God, and spoke to all Christian people of all ages. We should let him speak to us today, remembering that a blessing is promised to the one who reads; and to them that hear and keep the things that are written within this prophecy.

3. The book of Revelation is an apocalypse. Apocalyptic writings were, for the most part, produced in times of persecution. The apocalypse is always a writing of consolation and encouragement. It is an unveiling, a revealing, bringing comfort and increased courage to God's people who are undergoing great trial. The book of Revelation was produced in a period of persecution, probably during the closing years of the Roman Emperor Domitian, A.D. 95-96. The visions recorded in the book were seen on the island of Patmos, off the southwest coast of Asia Minor. John, the writer, was there in exile because of his loyalty to the word of God and the testimony of Jesus Christ. The writing is addressed to the seven churches of the Roman Province of Asia—the churches of Ephesus, Smyrna, Pergamum, Thyatira, Sardis, Philadelphia, and Laodicea. The number seven signifies completeness. This indicates that the book is addressed to the whole Church, the Church of the first century, and the Church of all centuries.

The Revelation was written in a time of great peril and persecution. There were dangers within the Church and perils without. The struggling young churches throughout Asia Minor, like torches flickering in the darkness and welter of a storm-tossed night, were ringed around with enemies. The Roman Empire, with all the resources at its command, was determined to crush them and still their witness which was threatening the ruin of the dominant political and social forces of that day. Many of the Christians were disheartened as they saw themselves surrounded by bitterly hostile Jews and subject also to pagan persecutions, in many cases even unto death. Throughout the book we find echoes of the deadly conflict. The followers of Jesus were faced with the choice between the worship of Caesar and the worship of Christ. This fact is made especially clear in the latter half of the thirteenth chapter, where we have the picture of some religious fête in honor of the emperor. The whole pagan population of the city is present in fanatical holiday spirit.

An image of the emperor is set up. Pagan priests and magicians work "miracles" to deceive the people; and by the art of ventriloquism the image of the emperor is made to speak and command that those who refuse to worship should be put to death. The frenzied mob of devotees of the imperial cult would not be slow to carry out this command. The peril in which the Christians were placed would not end with the passing of this public performance. Decrees were issued against them. They were slandered, proscribed, and continuously persecuted. They were a hated sect; and at any time some spy of the government or some personal enemy might lodge an accusation against them, and they were faced with the alternative of worship of the emperor or the charge of disloyalty and rebellion. "The native priesthood left no inducement—religious, mental, social, commercial—unused to break or wear down the constancy of the followers of Jesus, and to compel them to render at the imperial altar the worship that was regarded as the first duty of a loyal citizen."[2]

Darker days lay before the Christian community. Their hearts were filled with fear, and their own spiritual vitality was at a pathetically low ebb. They needed a renewed spirit of devotion, courage, and loyalty to Christ; a new baptism of faith and fidelity to fit them for their trials and temptations, both present and future. They and the Christians of all ages needed to be shown that conflict is inevitable, that we climb the steep ascent of heaven through peril, toil, and pain, but that after the conflict comes the victory.

The book of Revelation, therefore, an apocalyptic writing produced in a period of persecution and of great peril, is an unveiling, a revealing of Jesus Christ. He is shown to be present and powerful in the Church, in the world, in history, moving forward in steady progression for accomplishment of the eternal and holy

---

[2] Dean, *The Book of Revelation.* Used by permission of Charles Scribner's Sons, publishers.

purposes of God. He is not enshrined in the past; He is not shut up in history or in heaven. He is the eternal contemporary, let loose in the world where neither Jew nor Roman, man nor demon, can stop His progress. In His commanding presence men grow strong and effective, and the Devil and all his works go down before them. There are passages in the New Testament where the Apocalypse of Christ refers to a definite appearing at the end of the age. Such, however, is not the meaning of the title of this book. Here Christ is uncovered and revealed to contemporaneous human view. He will come in particular appearing at the end of the age; but here He is revealed as present and acting now, inspiring, strengthening, and leading His faithful followers to the final victory.

4. Apocalyptic writings are characterized by the use of symbols and highly figurative language. Among writers of this type of literature there was developed an elaborate system of cryptic symbols and figures of speech for the expression of spiritual ideas. An empire was symbolized by a wild beast, as in the prophecies of Daniel, an angel by a star; men were spoken of under the figure of animals. It was necessary for the apocalyptist to use images and expressions which would not be easily understood by the uninitiated. He was faced by the necessity of using language with a double meaning. He had to paint the unpaintable, see the invisible, and express the inexpressible. The apocalyptic writing, therefore, is full of imagery and symbolism which are hard to understand, and which make the task of the modern interpreter exceedingly difficult.

Symbolism is the representation of qualities, ideas, principles, by the use of symbols. The symbols have a hidden meaning, known only to the initiated. When a modern American boy says to another, "I will take you apart and lose some of the parts," he is using symbolic language which a first-century reader, unacquainted with the mechanism of today's jalopies, would find exceedingly difficult to interpret. A prisoner in one of our penitentiaries was there, according to his own statement, for having "bumped off a bird down in Alabama." The safe blower's "soup" is not the soup served on our dinner tables; and a gunman's "rod" does not come under the usual dictionary definition. These are illustrations on a low level of symbolic language, language with a double meaning. Literature of higher type abounds in symbols, picture writing, vague and entrancing suggestions rather than precise and clear-cut statements of fact. The apocalyptic writers by compulsion of the unsympathetic and often hostile environment in which they and their readers lived developed a system of symbols, figures, and codes by the use of which messages could be conveyed in comparative safety. A given passage might have two or more meanings, one for the casual reader, and another far deeper and more significant for the reader familiar with the figures used. This fact, as already indicated, adds greatly to the difficulty of interpretation, and effectually inhibits the discriminating student from basing dogmas upon symbolic passages. You cannot interpret symbols as you interpret simple prose, the meaning of which lies on the surface.

There is a difference between picture writing and symbolic writing. The Chinese writing was originally pictorial. In many of the characters which make up the written language, and which have undergone great transformation since writing began among the Chinese, one can still clearly see the picture of the thing represented. Symbolic writing, on the other hand, does not paint pictures. It is not pictographic but ideographic. The Indian sign of the arrow dipped in blood was not a picture but a symbol of war, just as three arrows in a tree was the symbol of an enemy. The skull and crossbones on a bottle of medicine is a symbol of poison, not a picture. The peacock, the phoenix, the serpent, are not pictures but symbols, respectively of immortality, the resurrection, and Satan. The ship is not a picture but a symbol of the Church. The fish, the lamb, and the lion are all symbols of Christ, but never to be taken as pictures of Him. In other words, the symbol is a code word and does not paint a picture. One must understand the code in order to read the symbolic writing. Jesus frequently spoke in pictures; and we can see the thing He presents, e.g. in the story of the prodigal son, the shepherd who lost a sheep, the woman who lost a coin, the parable of the sower. These and many other stories of Jesus present a perfect picture which can be put on canvas.

The book of Revelation has very few pictures, but it is full of symbols. In the first chapter we have a symbolic presentation of the Church and of Jesus: "I saw seven golden candlesticks; and in the midst of the candlesticks one like unto a son of man, clothed with a garment down to the foot, and girt about at the breasts with a golden girdle. And his head and his hair were white as white wool, white as snow; and his eyes were as a flame of fire; and his feet like unto burnished brass, as if it had been refined in a furnace; and his voice as the voice of many waters. And he had in his right hand seven stars: and out of his mouth proceeded a sharp two-edged sword: and his countenance was as the sun shineth in his strength." (1:12-16.) Here each part of the symbolism has a very definite meaning, but a picture of Christ as thus presented would be grotesque and meaningless. Throughout the book there are symbolic presentations, which even a cubist of the post-impressionist school of art could not picture on canvas. A beautifully expressive symbol is that of a lamb sitting on a throne. As a mere picture it would be ludicrous, but as a symbol we have the grace and gentleness and tenderness of the lamb and the power and dominion of a great throne. In the twelfth chapter we read of a great red dragon, having seven heads and ten horns, and upon his head seven diadems. The most daring artist would not attempt to draw a picture of that. It is not a pictorial but a symbolic description of the Devil. And so in chapter twelve the sun-clothed, star-crowned woman is not a picture but a symbol of the Church. For the most part the symbolism of the book is non-picturable. The writer employs these symbols as a method of communicating his thoughts to those who could read the symbols, and at the same time concealing his ideas from those outside the Christian circle. The meaning of the greater part of the symbolism of Revelation is quite clear to the modern reader; but there are also symbols in the interpretation of which there is much room for diversity of opinion, and about which one cannot afford to be dogmatic.

5. The symbolism of numbers. Even a casual reading of the Revelation impresses one with the frequent recurrence of certain numbers which have a symbolic significance. A. H. Baldinger, in his *Sermons on Revelation*, has a chapter on "The Arithmetic of Revelation," in which he points out that with the Oriental religious writer it was a common practice to set forth moral and spiritual truth under the symbolism of numbers. In earlier years when language was limited and vocabularies insufficient men fell back upon the use of numbers for the expression of ideas. A certain number would suggest a definite concept. Numbers became the symbols of ideas. Such numbers, obviously, cannot be read with the literal exactness that we employ when interpreting mathematical formulae.

The number *One* represents the idea of unity. It stands for that which is unique and alone; that which is independent and self-existent; the Alpha and Omega. The Hebrew thought of God as "one," so also the Christian and the Mohammedan. He is the unitary, the alone, the self-existent, the independent one. The number one does not occur symbolically in the book of Revelation. The following numbers, however, do appear, some of them quite frequently.

Two meant companionship, added courage, increased strength. In primitive days when men lived in the midst of dangers, constantly exposed to attack, there was comfort and courage in companionship. "Two were far stronger than twice one." And so the number two came to stand for added strength, increased energy, multiplied courage. There was a symbolic significance in the fact that Jesus sent forth His disciples two by two. Two witnesses confirmed the truth and their testimony was made strong. In the Revelation the truth of God is attested by two great witnesses who are slain and rise again and ascend to heaven. (11:3-12.) In chapter thirteen there are two beasts mutually confirming and supporting each other. The number two means increased strength, added power, redoubled courage.

Three may be spoken of as the divine number. To the primitive man, says Dr. Charles F. Wishart, home was the divinest thing that life had to offer. "Long before there was any authentic revelation of God, he found God in the interplay of love and kindness and affection in his own household. There was the father, with paternal love; and the mother, with maternal love; and the child, with filial love. No wonder that he began to think of the number '3' as the symbol of the divine. What wonder that there appeared glimmerings of a Trinity not only in the theology of the Hebrew but in the dreams of the Greek! You hear that three-chord note in Plato, and you overhear it again and again in the progress of the Bible. The divinest thing in human life was three, and the divine origin of life was three."[8] Three thus came to be the symbol of the Trinity— God, the Father, the Son, and the Holy Spirit. In one of the Roman catacombs there is a marble figure of Saint Cecilia, patroness of music, who is said to have suffered martyrdom in the third Christian century because of her refusal to sacrifice to idols. On one hand of the recumbent figure three fingers are stretched out, testifying in the hour of death to her faith in the Holy Trinity. Three carries the thought of the divine.

Four is the cosmic number. Primitive man had no conception of the world as we know it. To him the earth was a great flat disk with four boundaries, north and south, east and west. His first house probably had four sides; and when cities evolved he surrounded him-

[8] From *The Book of Day*. Used by permission of Oxford University Press, publishers.

self with four walls. There were four winds coming
from the four corners of the earth, and controlled by
four guardian spirits or angels. The number four became the symbol of the world in which he lived. In the
Revelation there are four living creatures, representing
all nature, all creaturehood; four angels stand at the
four corners of the earth, controlling the four winds of
heaven; four angels are bound at the Euphrates until
the moment comes for their work of slaughter. There
are the four horsemen of the Apocalypse, representing
the forces which go forth in history. The earth on
which man lived and worked and died was symbolized
by four. It stands for the visible creation.

Ten is one of the favorite numbers of the Revelation. It has been suggested that our decimal system
originated with man's study of his fingers and toes, just
as the baby begins its earliest study of itself. In primitive days there were men who through accident or warfare had lost one or more of their fingers or toes. They
were crippled and incomplete. The man who had five
fingers on each hand and five toes on each foot was a
full-rounded man. His members were complete. And so
the number five, doubled to ten, as on the intact
hands and feet, came to symbolize human completeness. The whole duty of the naturally complete
man is summed up in ten Commandments. In the Revelation the dragon and the first beast (chs. 12-13)
each have ten horns; and so also has the scarlet beast
(ch. 17) whose horns are interpreted as ten kings. The
ten horns are the symbol of complete power in government. As a multiple, ten occurs also in most of the
higher numbers of the book.

Seven is the predominant number in the Revelation,
occurring fifty-four times. It is a combination of the
numbers four and three, for primitive man soon
learned to add. He took three, the divine number, and
added it upon four, the cosmic number; and the result
was seven, the symbol of perfection—"the four-square
world plus the divine completeness of God." The number seven is earth crowned with heaven, the symbol of

perfection. The Babylonians regarded seven as the symbol of perfection or completeness. The Sumerians equated seven and "all." "The seven-storied towers of Babylonia represented the universe."[4] The book is addressed to seven churches—i.e., the whole Church—which are represented by seven lampstands and whose "angels" are seven stars. There are seven spirits of God. The book in the hand of God is sealed with seven seals; the Lamb before the throne has seven eyes and seven horns. There are seven angels with seven trumpets; and seven other angels pour out seven bowls full of the seven last plagues. Again and again the number seven occurs.

Twelve stands next to seven in the frequency of its use. Twelve is four multiplied by three. It is the symbol of organized religion in the world. The Old Testament has the twelve tribes of Israel, and in the New there are twelve apostles. The mother of Christ is crowned with twelve stars; and there are twelve gates to the Holy City. The New Jerusalem has twelve foundation stones, on which are engraved the names of the twelve apostles. The tree of life bears twelve manner of fruits.

Multiples of seven and ten and twelve are also of frequent occurrence. In early ages man took ten, the symbol for the idea of human completeness, and multiplied it by seven, the symbol for divine perfection. This gave *seventy*, the intensified symbol of perfection—"completeness that is not only human but divine." To the Jew seventy seems to have been a very significant number. There were seventy members in the high Jewish court. The Jews believed that there were seventy nations outside of Israel, with seventy languages, and under the care of seventy angels. Jesus sent forth seventy disciples. (Luke 10:1.) When He wished to express the idea of unlimited forgiveness He took the number seven, representing perfection, and multiplied it by seventy—"seventy times seven." This, of course, does not mean exactly four hundred and ninety times. Primitive

[4] *International Standard Bible Encyclopedia.*

man also took *ten*, with its suggestion of human completeness, and multiplied it twice—ten times ten, times ten, *one thousand*—to express the thought of ultimate completeness. A thousand years, the "Millennium," which occurs in the highly symbolic twentieth chapter of the Revelation, and nowhere else in the Bible, is not to be read with mathematical accuracy. It does not mean exactly one thousand times three hundred and sixty-five days, five hours, forty-eight minutes, forty-five and a fraction seconds. It means no definite period of time, and to interpret it with the exactness of the mathematician is to violate the entire law of symbolism in accordance with which the apocalyptic writer records his vision. *One thousand* means completeness raised to the highest possible degree—ultimate completeness. It means a period of time stretching over untold generations of unknown length. The number is not mathematical but symbolical.

Three and a half is another number that occurs frequently in the Revelation. Seven is the symbol of perfection; and three and a half, one half of seven, is the symbol for imperfection, incompleteness. This broken seven is a symbol of the interruption of the divine order of things by the devices of Satan and the malice of evil men. It stands for "restless longings not yet fulfilled, aspirations unrealized, the 'hope deferred that maketh the heart sick.'" The two great witnesses to the truth of God testify for three and a half years (11:3); the outer courts of the temple are trampled down by the ungodly for three and a half years (11:2); their dead bodies lie in the streets unburied for three and a half days (11:9); the spirit of life enters into them and they rise again after three and a half days (11:11). The saints of God are persecuted for three and a half years (13:5); the Church was in the wilderness for three and a half years (12:6; 12:14). "Always '3½' stood for the restless, the dissatisfied, the incomplete, for truth on the scaffold and wrong on the throne, for patient waiting until the dawning of the day-star in the eastern sky."[5] To try to calculate the chronological length of a three and a half period of time is to waste one's effort in a hopelessly futile task. It signifies the age of persecution, of imperfection, of hopes unrealized, whatever its length may be. Three and a half is half the period of sacred completeness.

There were also sinister numbers among the Jews, just as with us the number *thirteen* is for many people a number of evil portent. Some people will not sit down with thirteen at a dinner table. Many of our sky-scraper buildings have no thirteenth floor, and there is no room numbered thirteen in our hotels. There is a prejudice in the minds of men against this mystic number of evil significance. So also to the Jews there was a sinister significance in the number *six*. *Seven* is the symbol of perfection, and six falls short of the mystic seven and fails. Six signifies inability to reach the sacred height. For the Jew the number six had in it the very sound of doom. Since six has in it the sound of the stroke of doom, triple the six and you triple the doom. Three mysterious sixes—the very enunciation of the words carries the sibilant hiss of the serpent. Six hundred and sixty-six—this is the number of the beast (13:18); and this number is not a cryptogram, but a symbol. It stands for evil raised to the nth power—evil in its ultimate ascendency. Interpreters of the Revelation have exhibited an amazing amount of ingenuity and patience in trying to refer this number of the beast to some particular man in history. It stands for no man. It stands for a potency of evil than which no greater can be conceived. Not the name but the number is the important thing. "His number is Six hundred and sixty and six." The words make man tremble. There is in them "a depth of sin and a weight of punishment which no man can 'know' but he who has committed the sin and shared the punishment." There is, therefore, no possibility of finding the name of the beast in the name

[5] Wishart, *The Book of Day.* Used by permission of Oxford University Press, publishers.

of any single man who has appeared upon the stage of human history.

Six falls short of the sacred seven. It is failure to pass from the stage of incompletion where evil has the upper hand and go on into the full freedom and perfection of the sons of God. Failure to reach the best is six, it is sin. So also, in the final issue of things, sin is failure. In the symbolism of numbers there is great comfort in the fact that sin is six. It fitly represents the failure of sin to reach the goal of completeness to which it aspires. Sin never reaches seven. "Wrong and sin and selfishness can never attain ultimate victory." There are periods in world history when darkness rests upon the face of the earth and men's minds fail them for fear; when it seems as if the power of evil were permanently on the throne in the midst of human affairs. But this can never be of unbroken duration. Evil bears upon its own brow the mark of doom. Seven is victory; six is defeat. Sin multiplies itself on the level of six, but it never reaches *seven*. The bestial principle will never reach its full development. That principle is by the writer of the Revelation personified and marked with the number of doom; and he it is whom the Lord Jesus shall slay with the breath of His mouth, and bring to nought by the manifestation of His coming. The beast seen by John is still on the field of history. The warfare of the saints goes wearily on; but the ultimate victory is sure.

> "Though a mighty foe assail thee,
> Do not let thy courage fail thee.
> Soldier, do not yield,
> For God is on the field."

From what we have said of the symbolic use of numbers it follows that the numbers which occur in the book of Revelation cannot be understood with their real numerical value, nor even as round numbers. They are pure symbols, and we should discard our modern mathematical ideas and seek to discover their symbolic significance. Much of the unscriptural dispensational thinking of our day is based upon a false view of the value of the numbers which the writer of this book employs. John is an inspired poet, not an expert in millenarian mathematics.

2. *The Purpose of Revelation*

The writer of the Revelation, using the apocalyptic method in a writing enriched by highly figurative and symbolic language, gives us his philosophy of history. The fundamental principle in that philosophy is his profound faith in God and His righteous government, and in the ultimate triumph of the cause of Christ. The book of the world's history is in the hand of God. He is absolute sovereign upon the throne of the universe; and only Christ can take and open that book, unroll and interpret its events, and carry its program on to completion.

The Christians of that generation were in the midst of an alien, hostile environment; and in a period of unprecedented persecution. The present was characterized by chaos and confusion, ruin was around them, and the future seemed impenetrably dark. To the ordinary observer it seemed as if the Church and all it stood for would be utterly crushed, and that this community of those who followed Christ would be driven into denial of Him or done to death. John, however, with eyes that can see, looks beyond the borders of the visible. He lifts for his companions in tribulation the veil that obscures the far vision. When the hearts of others are failing them for fear, he sounds a clear note of confidence and of sure victory. The golden age, he tells them, is not behind us, the best is yet to be. He gives the Christians of his age a forward view. He puts prospect in the place of retrospect; and lifts men's minds to a vision of

"That God which ever lives and loves,
  One God, one law, one element,
  And one far-off divine event,
  To which the whole creation moves."

The joys and sorrows of life, the pain and persecution of the present, are not without meaning. They are only parts of a great plan whose design for the moment we may be unable to see; but the plan is there, and back of it all is God. The present may be dark and troubled and our minds perplexed, but John calls upon the future to carry his readers courageously over the present.

"Yesterday and today are heavy with labor and sorrow,
 And I should faint if I did not see the day
 That is after tomorrow.
 And so for me with spirit elate
 The mire and the fog I pass through;
 For heaven shines beyond the gate
 Of the day that is after tomorrow."

The book of Revelation, says Dr. C. A. Smith,[6] is the Christian epic of the day that is after tomorrow. The author admonishes his readers not to be forever imitating the example of Lot's wife and looking behind them—or around them: Look ahead, he says. Think of where you are going instead of where you have been, or now are. Things are bad today, but don't act as if the heavens were falling in bits of blue plaster around your feet. "By God's will doubt not, the last word is still Victory." The best is yet to be—so

"Keep a-goin', die a-tryin',
 Never give out;
 No pathetics,—quit your cryin',
 Trust, don't doubt.
 Eyes front, 'live and kickin',
 Don't squeal or squawl.
 Stick it out and keep a-stickin',
 Run, walk,—or crawl."

The first word of the book is the key to its content and purpose: *Apocalypse*, revelation. This word means

[6] *Keynote Studies in Keynote Books of the Bible.*

uncovering, unveiling. Christ is unveiled and the future of the Church is unveiled. *Unveiling* is the key to the book. That word opens wide doors and magnificent visions of conflict and victory and great glory appear. The unveiling of Christ, the final truth about Christ and His Church, that is the purpose of the last book in the Bible. And in this book we have the unveiled Person, the unveiled program of His purpose, and the unveiled power. The central truth which the writer seeks to impress upon the minds of his readers is that the world and all its events and affairs are under the control of Christ. History, with all its powers and forces, is under His direction; and He will ultimately bring about the full and final victory of good. He shows that the conflict between God and Satan, between good and evil, is inevitable, persistent, prolonged. The Church is in the wilderness, meeting with opposition, enduring persecution; but Christ is present with the Church, the source of her life and the assurance of her ultimate victory. Evil for the present seems regnant, but it is only for a time, and times, and half a time. The final triumph of God's purpose and the reign of His righteousness is certain. In the midst of persecution and peril the Christian should fear none of those things which he is called upon to suffer, but be faithful in his witness to Christ; and in the end he shall receive a crown of life.

And so the true Christian should be constantly looking forward. Of him it is true that hope springs eternal in the human breast; and, when the night is darkest, he may be comforted and cheered by the promise of the coming day. There is a divine conviction in the soul of the Christian which causes him to believe that when all human resources have failed and he is utterly helpless, then a Helper is on the way. When man's means are exhausted, God is coming; for man's extremity is always God's opportunity. To His suffering saints He gives grace sufficient for today.

> "He giveth more grace
> When the burdens grow greater;

He addeth more strength
When the labors increase.
To added afflictions
He addeth more mercy;
To multiplied trials
He multiplies peace.
When we have exhausted
Our store of endurance,
When our strength is spent
E'er the day is half done,
When we have come to the end
Of our hidden resources,
Our Father's full giving
Is only begun.
His love has no limit,
His grace has no measure,
His power has no boundary
Known to man,
For out of His infinite riches in Jesus
He giveth, and giveth, and giveth again."

The Coming of the Lord is the dominant note of the book. "Surely I come quickly" is the word of Christ to His suffering saints. That coming is a progressive and repeated coming. At many times and in many ways Christ comes. He comes when in faith we first turn to Him; He comes in the crises of life when we call upon Him; He comes in the hour of death to receive us unto Himself. All these and many other comings of the Lord, however, do not exhaust the full meaning of the promised coming of Christ. In the end, in the fullness of time, He shall come visibly in glory to close the scenes of our earthly history, and to usher in the final judgment. John reminds the readers of his day that the Lord is coming. He fixes our minds on this "blessed hope and appearing of the glory of our great God and Saviour Jesus Christ." (Titus 2:13, margin.)

Different writers have suggested many different themes which they think indicative of the central idea of the Revelation: The Coming of the Lord; Victory;

A Spiritual View of History; The All-Conquering Christ; The Son of God Goes Forth to War; The Unconquerableness of Christianity; We Climb the Steep Ascent of Heaven—all these and many more have been advanced as fitting titles for the book. One thing is certain: it is a book of supreme optimism. There is an undertone of assured hope running through every page. The Christian's Bible begins with a note of optimism: "And the evening and the morning were the first day"—first the evening, and after that the morning. (Gen. 1:5, K.J.V.) In history we pass through tragic sin and sorrow, suffering and death; there are moments of twilight and days of darkness; but we come at last to light—"for there shall be no night there." To the Church in the wilderness it is evening now; but we look for the morning, the morning of the eternal day. Alexander Maclaren many years ago said: "Because the day seems long in coming, let no man say it will never dawn. As we wait and watch, let us rather say how glorious will that noontime be of which the twilight dawn has lasted nineteen hundred years." That is the spirit of faith; that is the language of a man who sees Jesus and who is sure of the coming victory. We see not yet all things put under his feet, but we see Jesus, and our vision of Jesus is the promise and the prophecy of the coming victory. That is the thought that confronts us again and again in the Revelation. Lowell puts it thus:

"History's pages but record
    One death grapple in the darkness
  'Twixt old systems and the Word:
  Truth forever on the scaffold,
  Wrong forever on the throne,—
  Yet that scaffold sways the future,
  And, behind the dim unknown,
  Standeth God within the shadow,
  Keeping watch above His own."

The Church, with the risen, living Christ in the

midst of her, is to go into conflict. Her warfare in the world is inevitable. That warfare John pictures for us in all its tragedy. It is the tragedy of the struggle between right and wrong, and often wrong seems to be triumphant; but Christ is in the midst of the Church as she battles for the right. His presence and His power are in the Church's assurance of her ultimate victory. And so the Revelation is the symbolic story of the Church's journey through the wilderness of the world into the land of promise. The book opens with a vision of the radiant Christ in radiant glory. But soon the Church passes into the midst of persecution and darkness. "The mist of sin falls over the landscape. Then there is heard the noise of battle and the cry of pain, as storm after storm sweeps over the world." When we come to the close of the book, however, the storm has ceased, the clouds have drifted away, the warfare is over; the new day of peace and righteousness has dawned in splendor, and we stand upon the threshold of the New Jerusalem, looking in through the gates into the City of God.

In the Revelation there are two verses which are the key to the writer's primary message; and those two verses are easy to remember: 2:10 and 20:10. In the tenth verse of the second chapter we meet the Devil. In the following chapters we track the slime of his footprints through all the pages of history. His purposes are forever evil; his program is one of destruction and ruin; his hatred of God and of all good is hellish. In the tenth verse of chapter twenty, however, we see his end as he is cast forever into the lake of fire and brimstone. Throughout her history the Church of Christ has met with hatred, opposition, persecution. The Devil never rests in his warfare against the Church and the things for which she stands. The story of the Church is a story of unceasing conflict, but also of increasing victory; and in the end the Devil and all his works will go down before her, and she shall issue from the field of battle forever triumphant. That is the message of John and that is the Christian's sure conviction.

In general there are four theories of interpretation by which expositors of the book have sought to explain it.

1. The first theory is called the *Preterist*. This view looks back exclusively to the past and interprets the book as having to do only with the times in which it originated. It deals with a particular and dreadful period of persecution through which the Church of the first century was passing. The personalities of rulers, imperial and provincial, the policies of government, the persecution of the Church, the sufferings of the saints in that contemporary period, are pictured in symbols and under figures of speech which were intentionally vague to an outsider but perfectly clear and intelligible to those initiated into the current terminology of the Christian communion. The Revelation was a tract for the writer's time, and had a meaning and a message for his age; but for us today it possesses only an antiquarian and literary interest.

2. The second school of interpretation is called the *Futurist*. This view regards the book as almost wholly eschatological, dealing with the last things and the end of the world. It holds that by symbols and by definitely mathematical time periods the writer has given us a cryptic chart of the end of the age, the coming of the Lord, the rapture of the saints, the millennial reign, the loosing of Satan, the second resurrection, and the final judgment. Many sincere and devout men and women hold this view. To them the book is pure prophecy. What they call "the Church period" ends with chapter three; and from chapter four on all lies still in the future. Many of the advocates of this view are more interested in "the last things" than they are in present conditions. To some of them the book becomes very largely a problem in celestial mathematics; and they are more concerned with the calculating of time charts than they are in securing social and economic and political righteousness for their immediate neighbors. This school of interpretation generally holds that the events pictured in chapters four to nineteen

inclusive will take place within the brief space of seven years. This dreadful period of tribulation is the seventieth week mentioned in the familiar prophecy of Daniel 9:24-27, which seventieth week is separated by many centuries from the other sixty-nine and comes in at the close of the Christian era.

3. The third school of thought is called the *Continuous Historical*. Advocates of this view find in the Revelation a summary of the Church's history, a setting forth of that history in figurative and symbolic form, from the early days clear down to the end. The various symbols of the book are connected with definite historical persons and events, such as the invasions that overran the Roman Empire, the Saracens, the Turks, the Papacy, the French Revolution, the World Wars, etc. In other words, they find a chronological sequence in the visions of the book, a sequence which carries us across the field of history from the days of John down to the last day. The prophecies of the book are being continuously and successively fulfilled.

4. The fourth method of interpretation may be called the *Symbolic*. This view finds in the book the revelation of the great principles of the conflict between good and evil, of the increasing warfare between them, and of the final victory of the good. The symbols of the book and its mathematical numbers are not to be interpreted literally. They are spiritual disclosures—disclosures of the principles of God's government of the Church and of the world; and these principles are common to every age—past, present, and future. They are timeless.

There are elements of truth in each of the above views. Certainly much of the book belongs to the past. John was writing for his own generation, and he dealt with events and personalities of his own time. The persecuted Christians of that day would have found little comfort and encouragement in being told exclusively of what would happen at the end of the age, unmeasured hundreds of years beyond their generation. But John, in referring to the personalities and events of his own

day, undoubtedly had a wider, prophetic reference to
the events and personalities of other times. The principles revealed are essentially ageless; they belong to all
days. John considers the times in which he lives, and
he also considers Him who is above time. This is char-
acteristic of all prophetic writing, and John was a true
prophet. He does not make express predictions of persons and events which were yet hidden in the womb of
the far future when he wrote. He does not give in exact
chronological sequence the course of the Church's history in the world. He does, however, under the inspiration of the Spirit of God, disclose the secrets of God's
purpose and plan and method in the evolution of history. He reveals the great principles and forces which
are at work in the world; and he indicates the ultimate
issues toward which human affairs and the Church of
Christ are being guided. His visions related to contemporary events, but they are not limited to these. "History
is, in fact, one great echoing gallery where the present
re-echoes the past and anticipates the future." The
principles which controlled the history of John's time
control also the history of all times; and those principles
which the Revelation reveals are just as applicable to
our day as they were when the book was written. The
book has a message for us today; and we should divest
our minds of all fanciful schemes for charting the ages,
seize hold of its essential teachings and bring them to
bear upon the life of the Church as she confronts the
lost world today. The book of Revelation is a message
of God to the Church in any age.

Many different outlines of the book of Revelation
have been proposed—some of them based on presup-
position and fancy, some of them very suggestive. Dr.
C. A. Smith[7] outlines it as follows:

(1) The Church Hesitant, chapters 1-3.
(2) The Church Militant, chapters 4-20.
(3) The Church Triumphant, chapters 21-22.

[7] *Keynote Studies in Keynote Books of the Bible.*

For easy understanding of the general trend of the thought of the book, the following may be helpful:

(1) Christ Alone, chapter 1.
(2) Christ and the Church, chapters 2-3.
(3) Christ and the Conflict, chapters 4-20.
(4) Christ and the Conquest, chapters 21-22.

The outline which I prefer is, with some modifications, that followed by Moulton's *The Modern Reader's Bible*, which is built around the symbolism of the book and is an interpretation from the purely literary point of view:

The Prologue, a majestic Christophany and charge to the seven churches of Asia, covering the first three chapters, is followed by seven distinct sections, or visions, which begin with the fourth chapter and extend through the fifth verse of the twenty-second chapter. These seven visions are as follows:

1. The Throne, The Sealed Book, and The Lamb, chapters 4-5.
2. The Seals, chapters 6-7.
3. The Trumpets, chapters 8-11.
4. The Triumph, chapters 12-14.
5. The Bowls, Judgment Consummated, chapters 15—19:10.
6. The Word of God, Rider on White Horse, and the Throne of Judgment, chapters 19:11—20:15.
7. The New Jerusalem, chapters 21:1—22:5.

The Epilogue is in chapter twenty-two, verses six through twenty.

The conventional chapter divisions are retained here for the sake of convenience of memory, but they unfortunately break into the literary structure of the book. A more exact analysis necessitates a slightly different division of the verses, as is indicated in the following chapters.

CHAPTER II

THE PROLOGUE AND THE FIRST VISION

1. *The Prologue*

Revelation 1—3

THE PROLOGUE of Revelation consists of a preface
(1:1-3), an opening salutation (1:4-8), and the record
of a vision of Christ (1:9-20), followed by His charge
to the churches (chs. 2-3). In the opening words it
is stated that the book is "The Revelation of Jesus
Christ." The futurist school of thought interprets this
as meaning the revelation of Christ at His second
coming, to usher in a millennial reign. Sometimes in
the New Testament writings the Apocalypse of Jesus
Christ does refer to a visible appearing at the end of
the age (e.g., I Peter 1:7, 13). Such, however, is
plainly not the thought which John here has in mind. It
is a revelation made by Christ through His servant
John. Christ is the revealer, and Christ is the One revealed. He is here disclosed and uncovered to human
view, present in the world and in the Church. Here
Christ is the source of the revelation made to John. The
content of the revelation is the word of God, the testimony of Jesus Christ, and the things that John saw; and
a blessing is pronounced upon those that read and hear
and keep the words that are written within the book.
This book includes the final message of Christ to men;
and the benediction here pronounced upon the reading
and hearing of it is the first of the seven beatitudes
which the book contains: (1) "Blessed is he that
readeth, and they that hear the words of the prophecy,
and keep the things which are written therein" (1:3);
(2) "Blessed are the dead who die in the Lord"
(14:13); (3) "Blessed is he that watcheth, and

keepeth his garments, lest he walk naked, and they see his shame" (16:15); (4) "Blessed are they that are bidden to the marriage supper of the Lamb" (19:9); (5) "Blessed and holy is he that hath part in the first resurrection" (20:6); (6) "Blessed is he that keepeth the words of the prophecy of this book" (22:7); (7) "Blessed are they that wash their robes, that they may have the right to come to the tree of life, and may enter in by the gates into the city" (22:14). Thus in the very opening of the book we meet with the mystic number *seven*, and we have the beginning of a series of magnificent benedictions, opening with obedience to the revelation of Christ and closing with the entrance of the faithful into the Holy City of God.

The writer names himself, speaks a word of greeting to those whom he is addressing, and then tells of the circumstances under which the Revelation was received. He was on the isle of Patmos, in exile there because of his loyalty to the word of God, and the testimony of Jesus Christ. He was in exile and in tribulation; but he was also in the Spirit, and he heard a voice whispering within his soul. It was "on the Lord's day." (1:10.) It was on *Sunday*, the day of worship so full of sacred memories, the day upon which the Lord rose from the dead. And yet by a strange flight of fancy many interpreters understand these words to mean "the Day of the Lord." They tell us that John was lifted entirely out of his day and circumstances and transported into the far distant end of the age; and amid the stupendous scenes of that final day he sees the events and actors and their actions. John, as they believe, was in the midst of the scenes of the consummation of the Church's history. The book thus becomes a magnificent prophecy concerned wholly with the coming of the Lord, unrelated to those for whom John wrote or to us today, save as we try to unveil the mystery and read the signs of the times!

It was Sunday, the first day of the week. John under the inspiration of the Spirit heard a voice behind him, and turned to see. His turning to see was an indication of his receptivity to the revelation about to be given. Being turned, he beheld a dramatic and inspiring vision of Christ in the midst of the churches. As we consider this vision we must remember that John could give no literal description of what he saw. He had to fall back upon the use of symbols to represent the things that he saw and to express the impression made upon his mind. Madame Guyon, the French mystic, said, "God has an infinite desire to communicate Himself." By the use of symbolism the Holy Spirit here communicates to John a marvelous and enchanting vision of Christ. He saw the churches; he saw Christ; and he saw the messengers of the Church, the stars held in the hand of Christ. The vision of Christ dominates the whole book; and if we would understand the book we must also see and understand the vision.

First John saw the Church, symbolized by the seven golden candlesticks, in its relation to Christ and in its relation and responsibility to the world. It is a night scene, as is indicated by the presence of the lampstands and the stars. The world is in darkness; and the only light shining upon the darkness of the world comes from the Church. "I am the light of the world," and "Ye are the light of the world," said Christ to His disciples. The Church, the organized Christian community, is the medium through which Christ, the Light of the world, shines out upon and enlightens the world's darkness. The Church, therefore, is the thing of supreme importance in the world. The decrees of the Roman Emperor, the proclamations of the provincial authorities, and their subsequent persecutions seemed to the Christian of that generation the thing of supreme importance. But in exile, in a period of persecution and peril, John has a vision of the churches here and there in Asia Minor, flickering like feeble candlelights in the darkness and confusion of a storm-tossed night; and in the vision he learns that the thing of utmost importance in the chaos and confusion of the age in which he lived was the Church of the living Lord. The Church of Christ has always met with enmity and opposition; it

has always had its critics. We are living in an age today
when the criticism of the Church and its membership
and its works is one of the most popular pastimes. We
are told in book and pamphlet, in speech and conver-
sation, in newspapers and sometimes also in degenerate
pulpits, that the Church is a failure, that it has lost its
hold upon the hearts and minds of men. And yet
through the ages the Church has been the agency
through which Christ has been illuminating the
darkness of the world and meeting the needs of humanity. The Church has carried to the larger part of
the earth the good news of God's redeeming love and
grace in Jesus Christ. She has permeated human society and civilization with Christ's respect for personality, and has made His principles of the cross and of
individual and social righteousness more and more
operative in human affairs so that they are demanding
today a fuller and more concrete expression in the life
of the modern world. The Church has given to the world
the ideals of religious and political liberty, and racial
unity and social justice and human brotherhood.
Through the work of the Church and the convictions
which have come from her the most iniquitous of the
world's economic and social and political evils are
being driven into defeat or shamed into concealment.
The messengers of the Church have always been the
first pioneers and adventurers into the dark and neglected areas of the earth, in order that the people who
dwell there may come to know the richness of God's
blessing in Christ. The messengers of the Church, not
the militarists, not the magistrates, not the merchants,
have always taken the lead in the civilizing and enlightening work of the world. The messengers of the
Church, not medical men as such, have been the
first to go into all parts of the world with the science of
sanitation and physical healing. Not professional edu-
cators but the messengers of the Church have reduced
languages to writing, established schools, and set up
printing presses for the production of literature and the
distribution of the Word of God. Not social reformers

but the messengers of the Church have taken the lead in the fight against poverty, famine, and plague; and in the warfare against the evils of caste and custom. The Church has elevated the status of woman, created new conditions for childhood, established orphanages, asylums, and homes for the indigent aged and other unfortunate classes. And through it all the Church has proclaimed the tender mercy of our God whereby the dayspring from on high shall shine upon those who sit in the darkness and teach their feet to walk in the ways of peace. History affords no parallel to the unselfish and uplifting work of the Church. What goes on in parliaments and senates, in council halls and chambers of commerce, and in the supreme courts of the nations is always of importance to humanity. But when the world is out of joint, when men's minds are disordered and their hearts are failing them for fear, then the thing of supreme importance is the living Church, with all of her sanctuaries of worship and her avenues of service, where men come to have their faith strengthened, their thoughts clarified, their ideas uplifted, their convictions born, and their characters created. The Church is the institution of supreme significance and value in the world through all the ages.

The Church's capacity for shedding light depends upon the presence in her of Him who is Light. She cannot create light; she can only reflect the light, carry the light of Christ. No Church and no individual member of the Church can cast one ray of light upon the surrounding darkness save as they live in the light created by the presence of Christ. And so in the vision John sees Christ in the midst of the Church. Christ is in His Church today, and there is no need for much of the current pessimism. He is the center of her life, the source of her power. The function of Christ in the midst of the Church is suggested by His clothing— "clothed with a garment down to the foot, and girt about at the breasts with a golden girdle." (1:13.) Interpreters differ as to whether the clothing of Christ in the vision is the robing of the priest or that of the king with judicial authority. We prefer the latter view. The garment which Christ here wears is the robe of royalty, suggesting the right to govern and to judge. Christ alone has the right to pass sentence upon all the service that the Church renders. The girdle about the breast is the symbol of love and fidelity. "The King of love my Shepherd is." The judicial authority of Christ is exercised in "the faithfulness of eternal love. Every judgment He pronounces, every sentence He passes, is based upon love and patience."

Passing from the clothing of Christ we come to John's symbolic representation of the character of Christ. It is one of the most marvelous and suggestive portrayals of Christ ever given to the world: "In the midst of the candlesticks one like unto a son of man ... And his head and his hair were white as white wool, white as snow; and his eyes were as a flame of fire; and his feet like unto burnished brass, as if it had been refined in a furnace; and his voice as the voice of many waters. And he had in his right hand seven stars: and out of his mouth proceeded a sharp two-edged sword: and his countenance was as the sun shineth in his strength." (1:13-16.) Under the symbolism of these words we have the revelation of a sevenfold glory of Christ—seven points of perfection for the execution of His office and the exercise of His function:

(1) "His head and his hair were white . . . as snow." Two facts are suggested by the whiteness of His head and hair: the fact of His purity and the fact of His eternity. It is not the whiteness of age, for age is suggestive of decay, whereas Christ is eternally unchangeable. "All eternal things are pure," says Dr. Campbell Morgan, "and only purity can be eternal." Jesus Christ is the same yesterday, today, and forever. "His purity is the basis of His eternity, and His eternity is the crowning of His purity." The whiteness, therefore, is the revelation of the essential perfection and glory of Christ's character.

(2) "His eyes were as a flame of fire." This symbolism suggests His power to search the hearts of men and

to judge aright. His eyes are penetrative, they pierce the outer surface of things and get down to inner realities. He has infinite insight and infallible knowledge, nothing can be hidden from Him. "And there is no creature that is not manifest in his sight: but all things are naked and laid open before the eyes of him with whom we have to do." (Heb. 4:13.) One should stand in awe before the eyes of Christ, for the glory of God is burning in them. They see through and through. "There is no detail in the doings of the Church, or in the life of an individual member, that He is not perfectly acquainted with. He has seen and rightly valued every deed of lowly service for which the earthly records of the Church have found no place." Those who were with Christ in the days of His flesh were familiar with those flaming eyes, which could flash with quick understanding and, when need arose, burn with righteous wrath.

(3) His feet were "like unto burnished brass," as if refined in a furnace. Feet of brass suggest strength and stability. They symbolize progression, advancement, and indicate the inevitability of the procedure of the Son of man as He moves in the midst of the churches and leads in the march to victory. They have passed through the fire, which is symbolic of purification. "I will make the place of my feet glorious," saith the Lord (Isa. 60:13); and "How beautiful upon the mountains are the feet of him that bringeth good tidings, that publisheth peace, that bringeth good tidings of good, that publisheth salvation, that saith unto Zion, Thy God reigneth!" (Isa. 52:7). The Son of God goes forth to war; upon feet of purity He walks in the midst of the churches, seeing, knowing, and judging with divine insight; and His feet are of such stability that He can be hindered by no opposition.

(4) "His voice as the voice of many waters." We naturally think of the music and majesty of His voice. "The voice of Jehovah is powerful; the voice of Jehovah is full of majesty." (Ps. 29:4.) The simile would easily suggest itself to one who was listening to the

sound of the Aegean waves as they beat upon the
shore and broke about his feet. But more than this is
suggested by the figure that John uses in describing the
impression made upon him by the voice of Christ
heard in the vision. "God, having of old time spoken
unto the fathers in the prophets by divers portions and
in divers manners, hath at the end of these days spoken
unto us in his Son" (Heb. 1:1-2)—and the voice of
the Son is as the sound of many waters. It is the sum-
ming up of all the revelations given at sundry times
and in divers manners in the past. The many waters
come down from the past in many streams. Through
lawgiver and prophet and poet they come; but in Christ
they come together and unite, in Christ they mingle
and merge, and in Christ is heard the perfect harmony
of all God's great revelations from the past. There have
been many messengers and many messages—many
waters—in the unveiling of God's nature, in the disclosure of His will and His purpose for humanity; but
at last there is one Voice, one Word, and that is Christ,
God's full revelation and final speech to man.

(5) "In his right hand seven stars." These seven
stars are the seven messengers of the churches. (1:20.)
In the symbolism of numbers *seven* means *all*. All the
true ministers of all the churches are held in the hand
of Christ. They are ambassadors of the Great King.
They have no authority and no power in themselves.
They shall "shine as the stars," but for the holiness of
their office and the fulfillment of their function they
must be held in the light of the central sun. As Christ
moves in the midst of the churches He holds the ministers in His hand. This fact is an indication of the security and the authority of the messenger of the
Church so long as he remains submissive in the hand
of Christ.

(6) "Out of his mouth proceeded a sharp two-
edged sword." It is the sword of speech, suggesting the
penetrativeness of the divine word. "For the word of
God is living, and active, and sharper than any two-
edged sword, and piercing even to the dividing of soul

and spirit, of both joints and marrow, and quick to discern the thoughts and intents of the heart." (Heb. 4:12.) The sword of His mouth is the word of His warfare and of His judgment: "the word that I spake, the same shall judge him in the last day." (John 12:48.) All judgment, however, does not wait for the last day; and in the letters to the seven churches, in chapters two and three, we hear His word of swordlike speech as He pronounces judgment upon the life and the work of the churches.

(7) "His countenance was as the sun shineth in his strength." In this word we have a revelation of the essential deity of Christ. The Lord our God is a sun, and He will give grace and glory. (Ps. 84:11.) The faces of the righteous shall shine forth as the sun in the Kingdom of their Father. (Matt. 13:43.) The face of Christ, as seen in the vision, is a face of light and glory, shining in strength and beauty. So Saul in his vision of Christ on the road to Damascus saw a light above the brightness of the sun. The churches are the golden lampstands, the bearers of light in a world of darkness; the ministers are the stars; but Christ is the central sun. Christ is to the moral and spiritual world what the physical sun is to the natural world. Alfred Tennyson was standing in his garden by a bed of roses one day and talking with a skeptical friend. His friend said to him, "What does Christ mean to you?" Without a moment's hesitation Lord Tennyson, pointing to the flowers, said, "What the sun means to those roses."

Thus the risen, glorified Christ, Son of man and Son of God, is seen in John's vision of splendor. He is present with His Church on the earth, moving in her midst, seeing and knowing and judging with eyes of infallible insight and with piercing words of approval or of reproach. He is in the Church, the center of her unity and authority, the source of her life and power. There is, therefore, no room for discouragement as to the future of the Church. Christ's presence, His power, His wisdom, His faithful guidance and loving discipline, are the divine guarantee of the Church's ultimate victory. In chapters two and three we see Him in the midst of the churches on the stage of history, commending, complaining, and counseling, preparing them for the conflict with the forces of evil, and assuring the faithful of their final victory. The seven churches addressed actually existed in John's day, sources of light in great centers of heathen religion and culture. There were also other churches, fulfilling the same function, and these seven are selected as typical or representative of the whole Church. The seven letters are intended for the instruction, warning, and comfort of all the churches in all ages. For two of the churches, Smyrna and Philadelphia, there is nothing but praise. For two others, Sardis and Laodicea, there is nothing but censure. For the churches in Ephesus, Pergamum, and Thyatira both praise and censure are intermingled. This is a picture of the Church all through the ages. The idea that in these seven letters we have pictures of seven successive periods in the history of the Church—an idea familiar to readers of one of the most popular reference editions of the Bible[8]—is based on pure fancy. This interpretation is not found in the early Church, and probably was first suggested in the thirteenth century. According to the advocates of this view the seven churches of the book of Revelation represent seven successive stages of the Church's history. The church of Ephesus is the first period of Church history, that of Smyrna the second, etc.; and in these seven stages there is a setting forth of the ever-growing evil of the Church—her gradual apostasy. "These seven epistles are so many photographs of apostasy, taken at different periods of its life, from its infancy to its maturity"; and the predicted end of the visible Church is complete apostasy! This view is held by many sincere Christians; and yet it would seem to be in direct conflict with the clear teaching of Christ.

All history, even in its darkest and most disheartening periods, is moving steadily forward toward the ac-

[8] *The Scofield Reference Bible.*

complishment of God's eternal purposes. The ultimate
goal of history is a redeemed people, subject to the rule
of Christ as King of kings and Lord of lords. The ultimate victory of Christ's cause is one of the sure
teachings of Holy Scripture. The agency for the accomplishment of God's purpose is the living Church,
against which the world, the flesh, and the Devil shall
never prevail. The thing of greatest consequence in the
world is the Church. This was true in the first century
and it is true today. In John's day the world was in
chaos and confusion, the Church was under persecution, the world was against it, and it seemed to be in
dire peril. People's minds were perplexed. They were
asking, What shall the issue be? When shall we have a
better order of things? When shall we have a righteous
social system, a peaceful, warless world? When will we
see the promised city of God? John finds the answer to
these questions when the vision centers his attention
upon Christ and His Church. It was a poor Church, a
persecuted Church, a Church "too insignificant to find
mention in the annals of imperial Rome." It was, nev-
ertheless, the sole source of light in the world's
darkness, because Christ was in it. John, therefore,
puts this picture of Christ and His Church at the very
entrance upon the highway of human history.

In the letters to the seven churches the Holy Spirit
has in view the trials and conflicts which lay before
them. The letters are a challenge to conflict, to
"clear the decks for action." The Christians are urged
to rid themselves of everything that would hinder them
in their fight of faith. They must lay aside every weight,
every sin, every weakness of faith that could hinder
their victorious progress. "They must be their best, for
only then could they do their best." Christ is concerned
about the faith and life and work of the Church. He
opens doors of opportunity before her. On feet of
dreadful progression and holy power He moves in the
midst of her. Nothing escapes His eyes of flaming fire.
His words of swordlike judgment are pronounced upon
the Church's lack of love, her indifference to false

teaching from her pulpits, the godless life of some of her members, her neutrality and indifference to doctrine and to the great issues of the day. He sees with a penetrating insight and pronounces judgment upon all. He sees many a deed of lowly service which has never attracted the notice of men. He sees the widow with her two mites. He sees also the indifference and neutrality of the Laodicean Church, whose members are kindly tolerant because not interested in the great issues of time and eternity. He complains and condemns; He also commends and approves. "Cleanse yourselves," He says, "and be courageous. All of the promises and the power of God in Christ are yours. Therefore lift up your feeble hands and your palsied knees. Take up the burden of life gladly, bear it on bravely, and in the end lay it down triumphantly. And through all the varied experiences of life let the song of your soul ever be—

" 'Nearer, my God, to Thee, nearer to Thee,
E'en though it be a *cross* that raiseth me.' "

2. THE FIRST VISION: *The Throne, The Sealed Book, and The Lamb*

Revelation 4—5

BEGINNING with chapter four and running through the fifth verse of chapter twenty-two we have a series of seven visions, dividing the main body of the Revelation into seven distinct sections. In the last chapter from verse six to the end we have seven separate sayings, the seven final words of Christ. Thus the symbolism of the number seven runs through the whole book. The relation between these seven visions, 4:1—22:5, is not one of temporal succession. Each vision is complete in itself; and the relation between them is logical rather than temporal. They are like seven moving picture reels, showing the same thing from different viewpoints and increasing in climactic intensity. As we approach the main body of the book we should keep in mind the picture of Christ that we have in chapter one, the Christ who moves in the midst of the churches in chapters two and three. The Christ of the Revelation is not the Christ of modern liberalism. He is the Christ whom we see in the Gospels, the Christ of Bethlehem's virgin birth, of Calvary's cross, and of the open sepulcher. He is the Christ who makes men dissatisfied with themselves as they are and with the world as it is, and who tells us that through Him life may be transformed and the world overcome.

When we first glance at chapters four and five they seem like a strange and meaningless jumble of symbols. There are thrones and trumpets, jasper and sardius stones, and a rainbow round about the throne; there are four and twenty elders, and four multi-winged creatures full of eyes before and behind, and thunders and lightnings and a crystal sea; there is a seven-sealed book, and a lamb with seven horns and seven eyes. But back of the symbolism there is a beautiful and impressive meaning. In the preceding chapters we have seen Christ and the Church. We come now to the conflict of the Church, the story of the Church militant upon the scene of history. This conflict the writer will set before us in a series of visions, not chronologically successive, but each covering the whole period of the conflict from the beginning down to the end. Chapters four and five are anticipatory visions of the Church's anticipatory visions of the Church's final victory— preparatory to the actual commencement of the conflict. The Christians of that generation needed reassurance; and so in chapters four and five by the use of symbols the writer sets forth the existence, the power, the sovereignty, and the redemptive love of God. John and those to whom he writes are face to face with an actual throne, on which sat the Roman Emperor, "a monster in the shape of a man." He demanded the honors of the world and claimed the right to the worship of men. But in chapter four John sees another "throne set in heaven." (4:2.) The One who sat upon this throne was worshipped by all the inhabitants of heaven and all the creation of His own hand. The two thrones, that of the dominant world power and that of the Eternal God, are set in contrast; and the vision reveals that the throne of God is above the throne of Domitian. In chapters two and three we have a picture of things on earth. In chapters four and five we have a picture of things in heaven, a vision of the Almighty and Eternal who alone is worthy of the worship of men, and in whose hand is the book of the hidden history of the world.

The movement in this great vision of the redemptive power and love of God starts with the *throne* (4:2), moves by the way of the *cross* (5:6), and closes with every created thing brought beneath the sway of Christ. The twofold assurance of the ultimate accomplishment of the divine purpose of redemption is found in the *power* of God (ch. 4), and in the *love* of God (ch. 5). In chapter four is revealed to us the glory of God the Creator, and in chapter five the love of God the Redeemer. The revelation here reminds us of the words of Christ as recorded by John in the fourteenth chapter of his Gospel: "Let not your heart be troubled: believe in God, believe also in me." In the opening verses of chapter four we are taken into the throne room of the Great King, and hear Him say, "Believe in God." Then in chapter five we are ushered into the presence of the Christ of the cross, and we hear Him say, "Believe also in me."

At the beginning of chapter four John says: "After these things I saw ... a door opened in heaven." He did not see the opening of the door, neither did he know how it was opened; for "all revelation of spiritual things is a mystery. We cannot tell how it comes." But a door is always standing open in heaven, a door of access to spiritual things. Seeing the open door John also hears a voice, "as of a trumpet speaking with me." It was the same voice that he had already heard (1:10), the voice with the music and the majesty of many waters. The voice says to him, "Come up hither, and I will show thee the things which must come to pass." A very weird interpretation is given to these words by those who refer them to "The Rapture" of I Thessalonians 4:17. They are, however, simply an invitation to the seer to look at things from the heavenly point of view. John had been looking at the churches; the churches were looking at the Roman power which, with all the resources at its disposal, was threatening to crush them into submission to the imperial cult. Over against the powers of the world and all its forces of evil John was commanded to "come up hither" and see the infinite power and glory of God. We must see the things of earth, all the happenings of history, as they find their place in the purpose and plan of God and as they are held in control by the hand of God, before we can have any hope for the future of ourselves or of the world. "Come up hither" is Christ's word to His suffering servants in all ages. Look at things as they are seen from above!

John was obedient to the heavenly voice: "Straightway I was in the Spirit." The things of earth grew strangely dim, fading into the background. "Behold, there was a throne set in heaven, and one sitting upon the throne." (4:2.) God is on His throne. The throne is the symbol of sovereignty; and it is also the symbol of government. "Jehovah hath established his throne in the heavens; and his kingdom ruleth over all." (Ps. 103:19.) There are times when our minds are confused and we imagine that we could make a better world than God has. A Bohemian dramatist, Karl Capeck, has written a play in which he develops the idea that it would be possible to make a better race of men than God has made. He shows us the scientist in his laboratory making a new type of man—a man possessing all the qualities necessary for the doing of effective work, and yet having none of those qualities which make the workers of the world troublesome. There are today, as in John's day, those who believe they could create a universe, and arrange the course of human affairs, and make and manage men and women better than God has. But "Why do the heathen rage, and the people imagine a vain thing?" (Psalm 2:1, K.J.V.) God is still on His throne. He is sovereign in human affairs; He directs the destinies of individuals and of nations. His will is supreme.

John gives no description of the One upon the throne; and yet in verse three he employs the most magnificent and majestic symbolism to express the impression produced by the vision of God which he saw. He was "like a jasper stone and a sardius." The jasper stone of the Bible is a precious opalescent stone of divers colors. Here the descriptive words, "most precious" (21:11), suggest the diamond. It is the symbolism of the holiness and the glory of God coming into visibility. The sardius, a stone of carnelian redness, is the symbol of the awfulness of God's holy wrath. The rainbow about the throne is the symbol of God's covenant of grace, the reminder of His faithfulness. At the throne, majesty and mercy meet together. The whole picture with its symbolic stones beyond all price, and with the light shining through them, is a revelation of the holiness of God and His fiery wrath against sin. The emerald rainbow overarching the throne is the symbolism of mercy and hope in the midst of judgment—hope based upon the faithfulness of a covenant-keeping God.

Around this central throne are four and twenty elders, arrayed in white garments. (4:4.) These elders represent the Church in her future fullness. The number twenty-four covers the saints of the Old Testament and also those of the New—the twelve patriarchs or tribes and the twelve apostles. The number has no mathematical significance. It is the duplicated symbol for organized religion; and the elders represent the whole Church, the redeemed in glory. Their white garments are suggestive of purity; and in apocalyptic literature the white garment is the symbol of the resurrection body.

Four is the cosmic number; and the four living creatures of verses 6-8 are the symbol of all creation redeemed, transformed, perfected, and brought under obedience to God's will and manifesting His glory. Each of these living creatures has six wings, which wings symbolize the perfection of their equipment for the service of God. In vision, looking at things from the heavenly viewpoint, John peers into the far future and beholds all creation animate and inanimate serving and praising God.

These four living creatures and the four and twenty elders worship God because of creation. (4:9-11.) Their song is an anthem of creation: "Worthy art thou, our Lord and our God, to receive the glory and the honor and the power: for thou didst create all things, and because of thy will they were, and were created." (4:11.) This united hymn of praise is to "him that liveth for ever and ever." Earthly kings die and their policies pass away; but God is from everlasting to everlasting, and His faithfulness never fails. His word stands forever.

Chapter four, then, is a call to the Church upon the eve of conflict—a call to believe in God. This chapter, however, does not carry us beyond the Old Testament revelation of God. It discloses His majesty and holiness, His power and glory in creation. It declares that His sovereignty is above all earthly sovereignty. But God is not only Creator; He is also Redeemer. The All-powerful and the All-wise is the All-holy and the All-loving too. And so chapter five brings us over into the New Testament revelation of the God who loves and who redeems, the God "who loved me, and gave himself up for me." (Gal. 2:20.) The Christian believes in "God the Father almighty, maker of heaven and earth"; and he believes also in Jesus Christ, His only Son, who "suffered . . . , was crucified, dead, and . . . rose again." And so in chapter five we have unveiled to us the love of God the Redeemer.

In the right hand of Him that sat on the throne was "a book written within and on the back, close sealed with seven seals." (5:1.) There are various views concerning this book and its contents. It may be called the Book of Destiny. It contains the record of God's will and purposes for humanity. A will in Roman law bore the seven seals of the seven witnesses. The number seven indicates that it was perfectly sealed. The loosing of the seals signifies the unfolding of the course of history. No man was able to open the book or to look thereon. "The efficient factor in history" is not human force. No man can make history and no man can penetrate the secrets of the future. John weeps because he sees no human means by which the seals of the book can be broken and the world's destiny carried on to completion. The Church is the divine agency for the accomplishment of God's purposes, but the Church seems utterly impotent. How can its task ever be done? One of the four and twenty elders, seeing from above, knows that doubts and tears are unnecessary. "Weep not," he says; "behold, the Lion that is of the tribe of Judah, the Root of David, hath overcome to open the book and the seven seals thereof." Not a seal can be broken, not a single event can be brought into actuality, except under the guiding hand of Christ. "All history is in the hand that was pierced on Calvary." Only Christ, in His kingly character, can open the book and carry history onward to the final victory of the Church.

The book is placed in the hands of a Lamb, "standing, as though it had been slain." The efficient factor in history is the divine meekness and sacrifice of the Lamb of God. The Lamb has seven horns, which are the symbol of perfected power in government; and seven eyes, the emblem of the perfection of His penetrating and searching vision. He is omnipotent and omniscient. All power has been given unto Him in heaven and in earth. He is in the midst of the four living creatures and of the elders. "To Him all the works of God both in creation and in redemption turn." John had been told of a Lion, and he beholds a Lamb, the Lamb of sacrifice bearing the marks of the wounds in His glorified body. The Lamb comes and takes the book. This coming of the Lamb is God's manifest entrance as the final factor in human history. "He came" (5:7); God in Christ appeared upon the stage of humanity, and men beheld His glory. No man can read the record of what is not yet written in the world's history; and no man can direct the destiny of the world. But in the hand of God there is a book that holds the answer to the riddle of the universe, the solution to all life's problems and mysteries. The mind of man is baffled, but there is One who knows.

> "I know not where His islands lift
>   Their fronded palms in air;
> I only know I cannot drift
>   Beyond His love and care."

Christ, the Redeemer, takes the book; and all the problems of human life are answered in His work of redemption. The key to human destiny is in the hands of Christ: "Thou . . . didst purchase unto God with thy blood men of every tribe, and tongue, and people, and nation." And as we read the history of the world we see the hand of Christ unloosing the seals and unrolling the book. He is the solution to humanity's problems; He is the One Hope of the race. He is the center of the Bible, the center of history, the center of Christian experience, the Lord and Master of life. The book is never read for the satisfaction of human curiosity as to the future; but the seals are successively broken, and the scenes unveiled in their appointed order. To man the course of history is unknown, life with its problems is a seven-sealed book. The stone sphinx, lying for ages upon the sands of Egypt, is a symbol of the insoluble riddle of the world—"the world which at times is as terrible as a lion and at others as fascinating and inconsistent as a woman." But the Book of the World's Destiny is in the hands of the Lamb that was slain. He holds the power, and He unfolds the course of history, working out the will of God for the world and for the Church.

The living creatures and the elders worship because of redemption. They sing a new song, the theme of which is not creation but redemption, the self-sacrificing love of God in Christ. (5:8-10.) There is a responsive strain from the angels. (5:11-12.) They, too, rejoice with man and with creation redeemed and purified. Christ in the days of His flesh had told His disciples that there is joy in the presence of the angels of God over one sinner that repenteth. They rejoice here over the whole host of the redeemed. And then the whole universe takes up the song of praise, and we have the universal adoration of the Lamb who is King. (5:13-14.)

> "The whole creation join in one
> To bless the sacred name
> Of Him that sits upon the throne,
> And to adore the Lamb."

In verse fourteen the redeemed creation, symbolized by the four living creatures, closes the song with the sound of a grand amen. The glorified Church, represented by the four and twenty elders, with hearts too full for speech can only fall down and worship.

> "E'er since by faith I saw the stream
> Thy flowing wounds supply,
> Redeeming love has been my theme,
> And shall be till I die."

We have all sung those words, but the singing of God's redeeming love in Christ does not cease at death. The song carries over into the eternal world; and there "they sing a new song." Myriads of voices unite to swell the chorus—the song of the saved. There is the mingled music of voices of every tribe, and tongue, and people, and nation. The brown, the red, the yellow, the white, and the black sing together. Some of us may not be able to sing with our lips, but we can make melody in our hearts; and the harmony of heaven will sweep through our souls. Many of our old familiar songs, however, will not be suitable for the celestial chorus.

"Abide with Me," "Art Thou Weary?", "Almost Persuaded," "Lead, Kindly Light," and many others which we have loved from childhood cannot be sung in heaven. The hymnbooks of the Church on earth will need much revision.

Peter MacKenzie, the Durham miner who became a well-known Wesleyan evangelist, was accustomed to gather a crowd and get someone to preach to them. One day he assembled a large congregation, but the expected preacher did not come. The crowd began to urge Peter himself to preach; and finally he consented, saying, "If I must preach, give me my subject." "Preach about heaven," they said. In the midst of his preaching someone cried, "What do they do in heaven?" "One thing I know they do," he said. "They sing. I expect some day to walk along the streets of the eternal city and come face to face with David, playing on his harp and singing his own great song. I expect some day I shall lead the choir in heaven; and, if ever I do, there are two songs I am going to give out. One is 'My God and Father, while I stray'; and when I do someone will cry out, 'But Peter, you are in heaven now and you can't stray.' When they cannot sing that, I shall give out 'Though waves and storms beat o'er my head'; and when I do they will all shout, 'Peter MacKenzie, you are in heaven now and there are no waves and storms' . . . Then I think I shall stand in wonder and amazement, and say, 'What shall we sing?' And from all the heavenly choir will come the cry, 'Sing the new song, sing the new song.' Then all the redeemed in heaven, from the least unto the greatest, will join in singing praise unto Him who hath loved us and washed us from our sins in His own precious blood." The realism of Peter MacKenzie is the realism of the Revelation. Heaven is a place of beautiful realities and of song.

The central thought of this vision in chapters four and five is thus made clear. In chapter four we see the power of God the Creator; in chapter five we see the love of God the Redeemer. Chapter four says, "Believe in God"; chapter five says, "Believe also in me." Believing in the power of God and the love of God, there is no enemy, no force of evil, which the Church need fear. She can go into the conflict with the assurance of victory. The Almighty is still on His throne. The eternal God is thy refuge, and underneath thee are the everlasting arms. God has not laid aside the scepter of His dominion; He has not abandoned His throne to another. Faith in God steadies and calms one's mind; it is the essential condition of a proper evaluation of life and its issues. "One sat on the throne" which was above all thrones; and therefore chapters four and five are filled with songs of victory. The Church goes into her conflicts with a joyful confidence. Whatever may be her present outward fortunes, He who is with her is mightier than all the forces which are arrayed against her. He is the Creator, the ultimate source of all existence, all power, and all sovereignty. But the Christian assurance goes deeper than that. The Church can count on Christ and His accomplished work of redemption. Having loved His own which are in the world, He will love them to the end. From the realms of glory He stands and cries to His Church and says: "Let not your heart be troubled: believe in God, believe also in me." And in the end we see the saints, "safe penned in paradise," brought and bound together in the presence of the living Christ.

CHAPTER III

THE SECOND AND THIRD VISIONS

1. THE SECOND VISION: *The Seven Seals*
Revelation 6:1—7:17

THIS VISION begins with the cross and the going forth of the gospel (6:1-2), passes beyond the final judgment (6:12-17), and closes with the saints in eternal glory (7:9-17). In this section we see history evolving under the direction and control of the Lamb. In the preceding vision we have seen that back of all history is God in Christ; and here we see the hand of Christ opening and unfolding the sealed book of the world's destiny. "That Divine love is the motive power of history does not imply that all calamitous phenomena are absent, but that they are under Christ's control. And, therefore, there is no experience, however calamitous, but may be made to subserve man's redemption. 'All things are yours.'[9] With this vision the main action of the book really begins. Here we have the conflict and struggles of the Church, the judgment of God upon her enemies, and her final victory. Here are the four grim Horsemen of the Apocalypse, the four great combatants on the stage of history.

The vision opens with the breaking of the first seal, and one of the four living creatures crying as with a voice of thunder, "Come." This is the cry of the waiting creation, the longing for the manifestation of the Lord. The word "come" is addressed in each instance to the riders on the different horses; and is a call for the actors in the pageant to take their places, for the events and forces of history to unroll. In answer to the first

[9] Dean, *The Book of Revelation.* Used by permission of Charles Scribner's Sons, publishers.

call to "come," John saw "a white horse, and he that
sat thereon had a bow; and there was given unto him
a crown: and he came forth conquering, and to conquer." (6:2.) The personality represented by the rider
on the white horse has been a puzzle to many interpreters. To my mind the simplest and most harmonious
view is that which sees in this figure Christ Himself,
or probably the cause rather than the person of
Christ. The color of the horse is suggestive of heavenly
purity. The rider wears the crown of royalty; and he
carries a bow, the instrument of war with which he will
overcome his enemies. He goes forth conquering and to
conquer. There is here the representation of the continued victorious march of God's truth and the progressive judgments of history. The progressive advance
of the cause of Christ will continue, and in the end He
will leave no foe unvanquished. He rides forth for judgment on a wicked world, judgment which men have
brought upon themselves by their willful rejection of
the rightful and righteous King of humanity. The idea
symbolized may be expressed in other words by saying
that the victorious rider on the white horse represents
the victorious course of the gospel. The cause of
Christ, the Church of Christ in history, has not been a
failure, and it will not fail. The gates of hell shall not
prevail against it. The man who has lost faith in the ultimate victory of the Church has lost faith in God. If
we go back through the centuries since Christ became
incarnate in human history, go back century by century
and decade by decade, we see always the continued
victorious progression of the cause of Christ and His
Church.

But along with the white horse there go forth other
horses. The gospel conquers, but there are other alien
and hostile forces in history. The rider on the white
horse, however, has the power and the place of prece-
dence, and in the end will prevail against all alien
forces. When the second seal is opened, the second living creature cries, "Come"; and there comes forth a
red horse. (6:4.) This second horseman is war; red,

the color of blood, is the color of war. Peace is taken from the earth, and warfare follows. The war, however, is not between the righteous and the wicked, but among the wicked alone. They "slay one another." They have cast off the rule of the Prince of Peace. They are at enmity with the rider upon the white horse, therefore they lack the foundation of true brotherhood and are at enmity one with another. There will be no peaceful, warless world until the Prince of Peace has become the acknowledged King of humanity. When His rule is accepted, and His principles are operative in all human relationships, then the rider upon the red horse will be forever vanquished.

With the opening of the third seal there went forth a black horse. (6:5.) The horse and his rider here symbolize famine. Black is the color of gloom and mourning. The mourning is caused by famine, by the scarcity of man's essential food. This is indicated by the balances; for to give grain by weight instead of by measure was an indication of extreme scarcity. Under ceaseless, destructive war the fields have been made desolate and bare, and grain has increased in price beyond the reach of the poor. A day's wage of a common workman would purchase only enough coarse food for himself, allowing no provision for his family. (6:6.)

The fourth seal is opened and there comes forth pestilence. The color of the horse is "pale," a greenish yellow, the lurid color of a corpse. The rider on the pale horse is named Death. Death rides upon Pestilence. "Death the reaper is followed by Hades the garner." Death here has a significant meaning: it is not natural death, but death as God's judgment. Death and Hades execute the judgments of God upon the wicked in a fourfold manner—by sword, famine, death, and the wild beasts. (6:8.) The desolation wrought by them was to be only partial; they were to execute judgment over the fourth part of the earth. The earth desolated by war, famine, and pestilence is invaded by wild beasts.

"And so there grew great tracts of wilderness
Wherein the beast was ever more and more,
But man was less and less."

Thus war, famine, and pestilence ride forth in opposition to the cause of Christ, in irreconcilable enmity
to the blessed Rider upon the white horse, the King of
kings and Lord of lords. For unbroken centuries men
have been trying to make these four horsemen ride side
by side in peace; but it can never be done. There can
be no peace between Christ on the one side, and war
and famine and pestilence on the other. Either the
rider on the white horse will conquer the riders upon
the other horses or be conquered by them. Despite the
many failures of Christian people, they have gone a
long way in nineteen hundred years in the fight against
these three great enemies of the human race. War is
not as popular as it once was. We recognize the rider
upon the red horse for the vile and hateful thing he is.
Christian civilization has also fought a valiant and increasingly victorious fight against famine and pestilence. The poverty and hunger of the world are still
appalling. "Conservative minds shrink from anything
which smacks of social control." But unless the hungry
people of the world are fed, then our capitalistic systems are faced with the certainty of red revolution.
Christ who fed the hungry in the days of His flesh is
still "keeping lonely vigil while we sleep." There is no
need for grinding, degrading poverty in a world of
resources such as ours, if that world were regulated by
the principles of Christ. Medical science has made
wonderful strides in the warfare against the rider on
the pale horse, and is steadily lowering the mortality
rate in human life. And while we do all that we can,
under the inspiration of the Spirit of Christ, to fight the
good fight against physical death, there is still that
"deeper terror, the second death, the death of the soul.
Only the blessed Master of Life and Light who rides
on the white horse can overcome this final enemy." He
alone has shown us that the rider upon the pale horse

is only a phantom; and has taught us to say, "O death, where is thy sting? O grave, where is thy victory?"[10] In Him God has brought life and immortality to light, and enabled us to cry,

> "Because I know the spark
> Of God has no eclipse,
> Now Death and I embark
> And sail into the dark,
> With laughter on our lips."[11]

With the opening of the fifth seal (6:9-11) we come into a quite different region of thought, passing from the material realm into the spiritual. When the seal had been opened John saw "underneath the altar the souls of them that had been slain for the word of God, and for the testimony which they held." These souls are the souls of the martyrs slain in persecution. Their cry for vengeance is an expression of the moral difficulty involved in that God's judgment does not immediately fall upon those who have persecuted and done to death "the noble army of martyrs." Milton voices the same prayer for retribution and the vindication of the moral order of the universe when he cries:

"Avenge, O Lord, Thy slaughtered saints, whose bones
  Lie whitening on the Alpine mountains cold."

A white robe is given to them, the apocalyptic symbol of the resurrection in righteousness; and they are assured that the divine purpose and plan must be fulfilled. "Judgment cannot finally be passed upon the world till every phase of the world conflict be past, and God prove victorious through all. . . . In the end the complete triumph of God will be revealed. But when the individual's conflict is over, his victory is secured;

---

10 I Corinthians 15:55, King James Version.
11 From Joseph Plunkett's poem, *"The Spark,"* quoted by C. F. Wishart in *The Book of Day.* Used by permission of Oxford University Press, publishers.

and he has only to wait for the close of the great world battle."[12] There have been many dark periods in the world's history and in individual experience when devout souls have been constrained to cry, "How long, O Master, the holy and true, dost Thou not judge and avenge?" We grow impatient at the delays of divine judgment. But God measures time not as man; with Him one day is as a thousand years. The righteous suffer for the necessities of life while those who trample them under foot are possessed of prosperity, place, and power. "Fret not thyself," says the psalmist; for in God's appointed time they shall be cut down like the grass and wither as the green herb. In the end we shall understand, and then we shall praise God in the presence of all His doings and the delays of His judgment.

The opening of the sixth seal brings us to the great and terrible day of the Lord. (6:12-17.) We have here a picture of every great calamity by which a sinful world is overtaken; but specifically a picture of the chaos and upheaval at the second coming of Christ for the final judgment. The earthquake, the darkening sun, the reddening moon, the falling stars, the moving mountains and islands, symbolize the final shaking and breaking up of the world, and the terrors of the coming judgment. The terrified inhabitants of earth call upon the mountains and rocks to fall upon them and hide them from the face of Him who sits upon the throne, and from the wrath of the Lamb. They know at last that there is such a thing as the wrath of God for those who persist in willful and wicked rebellion against His holy will. "Even the swift agony of being crushed to death is preferable to being left face to face with the indignation of an outraged God." (Moffatt.) While, as indicated above, other judgments of God in history are not excluded, this sixth seal must be interpreted

---

[12] Dean, *The Book of Revelation.* Used by permission of Charles Scribner's Sons, publishers.

eschatologically; it brings us down to the end of the Christian era.

Now the central teaching of chapter six is clear. Truth seems forever on the scaffold and wrong forever on the throne; and our minds are sometimes filled with perplexity and doubt almost to despair. But "behind the dim unknown, standeth God within the shadow, keeping watch above His own"; and in the end it will be seen that His will is wise and His ways are just. The writer of the Revelation is dealing with the eternal principles, the essential characteristics, of God's government in the world and in the Church. John is looking at things from above; he gives us a superview of history. In his view, the centuries since Christ came and died and rose again reveal one great fact: "At every point at which we pause we see the Son of God going forth conquering and to conquer. We see the world struggling against His righteousness, refusing to submit to it, and dooming itself in consequence to every form of woe. We see the children of God following a crucified Redeemer, but preserved, sustained, animated— their cross, like His, their crown. Finally, as we realize more and more deeply what is going on around us, we feel that we are in the midst of a great earthquake, that the sun and the moon have become black, and that the stars of heaven are falling to the earth; yet by the eye of faith we pierce the darkness, and where are all our adversaries? Where are the kings and the potentates, the rich and the powerful of the earth, of an ungodly and persecuting world? They have hid themselves in the caves and in the rocks of the mountains; and we hear them say to the mountains and to the rocks, 'Fall on us, and hide us from the face of him that sitteth on the throne, and from the wrath of the Lamb: for the great day of their wrath is come; and who is able to stand?' "[13]

We would naturally expect the opening of the seventh seal to follow immediately upon the opening of

[13] Milligan, *The Book of Revelation.*

the sixth; but the saints need to be assured. The sixth
chapter closes with the question, "Who is able to
stand?" Chapter seven gives the answer.

> The soul that on Jesus hath leaned for repose
> God will not, no, will not, desert to its foes.

Before the opening of the seventh seal there is an anticipatory vision assuring the Church of her safety
through all the course of history, and specifically in the
terrors that will accompany the second coming of
Christ. Whatever happens the followers of Christ are
secure. Before the deepest darkness there is a word of
comfort. The righteous are sealed; they are marked as
God's. "The Lord knoweth them that are his." (II
Tim. 2:19.) In the first eight verses of chapter seven,
therefore, we have the sealing of the saints. The seal is
the mark of ownership, and the sign of divine protection. (Cf. Ezekiel 9:1-11.) In the midst of all the
upheavals of history, in the stress of the last dread
days, God's protecting banner of love is over them.
The number of the sealed is 144,000. This number,
however, has no exact mathematical value. It is purely
symbolical. The number twelve is first multiplied by itself, and then multiplied by a thousand; and this indicates the fact of the utmost completeness. The holy
catholic Church, the Church universal, all Christians,
are sealed and their safety assured. Not one member of
the true Church will be lost. Again the saints of both
the Old and the New Testaments are indicated by the
multiplied twelve. There is no distinction here between
the Jew and the Gentile; the Church of Christ is one.
There is a beautiful suggestiveness in the fact that the
sealing of the saints is done by an angel ascending from
the sunrising.

In the latter half of this chapter (7:9-17) there is a
vision of the Church's safety after the upheavals of the
great and terrible day; and we see the unnumbered
multitude of the redeemed in glory. John sees "a great
multitude, which no man could number, out of every

nation and of all tribes and peoples and tongues, standing before the throne and before the Lamb, arrayed in white robes, and palms in their hands; and they cry with a great voice, saying, Salvation unto our God who sitteth on the throne, and unto the Lamb." This is not a picture of the Church on earth, but in glory. The earthly pilgrimage is over, and the people of God have entered into their eternal rest. They have peace and joy and every want supplied. "Death is swallowed up in victory, and every tear is wiped from every eye."

In this second of the seven visions, therefore, we see the going forth of the gospel "conquering and to conquer"; we see all the movements of history and of nature—war, famine, pestilence, persecution, earthquake, and storm—under the control of God. Christ is the Master who in the end wins the victory over war, poverty, pestilence, death, and the world of the dead. He holds the keys. After all the conflicts and catastrophes of history are over there is seen the gathering of the redeemed, and the song of the saved in glory is heard. In his vision John saw in heaven "a great multitude, which no man could number," but God numbers and seals them all: "the very hairs of your head are all numbered." Tacitus, the Roman historian, wrote that by the year A.D. 64, during the days of the infamous Nero, the Christians were already an *ingens multitudo*, a mighty multitude. The rapid growth of Christianity during the first decades of its history is one of the marvels of the years. It was ridiculed, slandered, proscribed, persecuted; and the adoption of it was made punishable with confiscation of property and death. The followers of Christ were tortured, burned, mutilated, thrown to wild beasts. Yet the Church grew and increased in numbers and influence. Through the years that increase has continued. A recent government census in India shows that in that one land an average of four hundred Christians a day had been added to the Church during the preceding decade. "Are there few that be saved?" John answers that question: "A great multitude, which no man could number." A good many years ago Daniel Webster was traveling in the then uninhabited part of the West. Suddenly he stopped and bent his head and seemed to be listening. His companion, in surprise, said to him, "What are you doing?" "I am listening," he replied, "for the tramp of the coming millions." And so the ear of faith can feel the tremor of the earth beneath the feet of a mighty multitude of men and women and children—the great multitude of the redeemed:

> "They are flocking from the East
>   And the West,
> They are flocking from the North
>   And the South,
> Every moment setting forth
> From the realm of snake or lion,
>   Swamp or sand,
>   Ice or burning.
> Greatest and least,
>   Palm in hand
> And praise in mouth,
> They are flocking up the path
>   To their rest,
> Up the path that hath
>   No turning.
> Up the steeps of Zion
> They are mounting,
>   Coming, coming,
> Throngs beyond man's counting;
>   They are thronging
> From the East and West,
>   From the North and South;
> Saints are thronging, loving, longing,
>   To their land
>   Of rest,
> Palm in hand
> And praise in mouth."[14]

[14] Christina G. Rossetti. Used by permission of The Macmillan Company, publishers.

In verse fourteen one of the elders tells the seer who this multitude around the throne are: "These are they that come out of the great tribulation, and they washed their robes, and made them white in the blood of the Lamb." Victory and joy through struggle and tribulation is the message of the whole book. This word of the elder sums up the history of the Church—tribulation; and forecasts her future—victory. The tribulation itself, however, will not make the robes white. Affliction in itself does not sanctify. It was "the blood of the Lamb," the atonement of Christ, which made and kept them white. We are not told of this multitude when or where they were born and lived, nor how they died. We are not told whether during their days on earth they were wise or foolish, rich or poor, old or young. Of them all the only thing recorded is that they believed in Christ. "They washed their robes . . . in the blood of the Lamb." Faith in Christ is the fact enshrined in these words. That is the ultimate test; that determined their eternal destiny.

"Therefore," because of their faith in Christ, "are they before the throne of God; and they serve him day and night in his temple . . . They shall hunger no more, neither thirst any more; neither shall the sun strike upon them, nor any heat: for the Lamb that is in the midst of the throne shall be their shepherd, and shall guide them unto fountains of waters of life: and God shall wipe away every tear from their eyes." We are told that Robert Burns could never read these words without tears coming into his eyes. The Lamb is in the midst. Perhaps the first words which the author of the book of Revelation ever heard about Jesus were the words of John the Baptist when he pointed Him out as the Lamb of God. The Christ whom John sees in heaven is the Christ who walked in the wilderness of Judea and by the shores of the Galilean sea. Christ is here described also as the *Shepherd*—the shepherd of the lost sheep whom He has found and brought home. We shall not be left to explore the mysteries of the glory world and discover its riches alone. There we shall be still under the guiding hand of the Good Shepherd. "He who guided the outgoings of His first disciples amidst the hills of Galilee and by the lake shore, through the plains of Samaria and in the highlands of Judea, will guide the quests of the celestial city." In this world there are no eyes which have not been dimmed by tears; but there "God shall wipe away every tear from their eyes." All tragic and haunting memories will be forever banished from that holy place.

> "And now all tears wiped off from every eye,
> They wander where the freshest pastures lie,
> Through all the nightless day of that unfading sky."

Who can find words to express the glory of it!

2. THE THIRD VISION: *The Seven Trumpets*
Revelation 8—11

CHAPTER EIGHT begins with the opening of the seventh seal, followed by "a silence in heaven about the space of half an hour." It is a silence of "trembling suspense," a dramatic pause; a silence of reverence, expectancy, and prayer. What follows shows that this cessation of the voices in heaven is in order that the prayers of the saints may be heard. "The needs of the weakest saints on earth concern God more than the psalmody of the highest order of the heavenly host." It would seem that the opening of the seventh seal would reveal the consummation of all things and the final victory of Christ. The lightnings and thunders of the storm cease, the music of heaven is hushed; and we seem to have come to the very end of history's drama. But while the multitude of the redeemed awaits in eager expectancy, a new vision opens before us, and instead of Christ's eternal reign of righteousness and peace, we find ourselves looking down still upon a wicked and rebellious world, a storm-swept earth. The vision of the trumpets, like that of the seals, carries us

back to the beginning; and once more we move across
the weary and troubled course of human history. The
vision of the trumpets does not follow that of the seals
in chronological sequence. They are synchronous, each
covering the entire history of the Church, from the beginning of the Christian era down to the end.

Seven trumpets are given to the seven angels which
stand before God. The number seven is again to be understood in its symbolic significance. It expresses the
varied forms and at the same time "the essential
oneness of the action of Him to whom the Father has
given authority to execute judgment because He is the
Son of man." While these angels, representatives of the
divine Judge of men, stand ready to sound their
trumpets, another angel comes and stands at the altar,
having a golden censer, and there is given unto him
much incense that he should add it to the prayers of all
the saints. (8:3.) The time for the answering of the
prayers of the saints for God's judgment upon sin
(6:10) has come. God will vindicate the cause of the
righteous. The angel takes their prayers and adds to
them incense so that they may be seen ascending to
God to receive His answer. It is the symbolic assurance
that the prayers are heard. We have here also the assurance that all the prayers of all the saints of all the ages
are added to ours when we pray for the advancement of
the Kingdom and the manifestation of the King. In the
fifth verse the angel takes the fire of the altar and casts
it upon the earth: the prayers are heard and the fire is
cast that it may consume in judgment. Now the silence
is broken; there are thunders and voices, and lightnings
and an earthquake, which are the symbolic warnings of
the judgments that are about to descend. The trumpets
are warnings of judgment and calls to repentance; and
they are an answer to the prayers of God's people.

The sounding of the first trumpet brings blight upon
the land. (8:7.) The destruction produced, however, is
only partial—"the third part"; and that partial destruction is a solemn warning. Every judgment of God is a
call to repentance. The writer views the destructive

forces, the catastrophes of nature, not as a scientist but as a prophet. John is not a meteorologist. As an inspired poet he sees the hail and fire, and the burning of the trees and grass, as "manifestations of the mind of God"; and he describes them as judgments sent by God.

The first trumpet affects the land, the second affects the sea (8:8-9): "as it were a great mountain burning with fire was cast into the sea: and the third part of the sea became blood; and there died the third part of the creatures which were in the sea ... and the third part of the ships was destroyed." Interpreters have shown great ingenuity in trying to identify this burning mountain falling into the sea with some particular heresy in the Church, or some evil movement in history. They attempt to work out all the details of the symbolism and often reach absurdly grotesque conclusions. We should remember that symbols are not pictures; they are vast and splendid suggestions, appealing to the imagination. John is not referring to particular persons and events. He is simply giving us a symbolic and dramatic portrayal of the whole course of human history.

The third trumpet brings blight upon the rivers and fountains of the waters (8:10-11): "there fell from heaven a great star, burning as a torch, and it fell upon the third part of the rivers, and upon the fountains of the waters; and the name of the star is called Wormwood: and the third part of the waters became wormwood." Here the judgment is intensified: "Many men died of the waters." The waters of the world become the very essence of bitterness to their own votaries. One pleasure after another grows tasteless, one enthusiasm after another loses its thrill. A few years ago one of America's most distinguished cartoonists committed suicide. He had wealth and genius and fame and friends. Before taking his life he wrote a letter in which he confessed that he had gone from wife to wife and country to country in the vain effort to escape from himself; and that he ended his life because he was fed up with trying to discover ways of getting through the twenty-four hours of the day. The waters of the world had become bitter. "The irony of heaven weighs heavily upon me," was the confession of Heinrich Heine. Here again literalistic interpreters of the Revelation seek to identify the falling and burning star with some particular heretic or heresy. Simon Magus, Cerinthus, Arius, Pelagius, and others have been singled out for this unpleasant distinction. Some Protestants think of the falling star as Romanism. Romanism thinks of it is Protestantism; and fundamentalists think of it as modernism. John means none of these. In symbolism he is simply saying that the sin of the world carries moral and spiritual poison into the very springs of life; and that the waters of the world become bitter to the enemies of God.

The fourth trumpet (8:12) brings blight upon the light and a plague of darkness. This judgment upon the heavens makes the terror of the trumpet plagues universal—the smiting of the third part of the sun and the moon and the stars. There are periods in history when the world gropes its way in darkness. We are passing through such a period now. There have been times when the sun was eclipsed, when Christ was concealed when the Church was under a shadow, when the Bible was obscured, and deep darkness covered the face of the earth. But always a remnant remains, Christ lives on, the Church continues. Christ moves forever in the midst of His Church, and there will always be those who will keep the torch of truth uplifted and the light of faith still shining.

Now four is the cosmic number; and these first four trumpets bring judgment upon nature. The forces of nature are all under the control of God. Thunder and lightning, storm and tempest, fire and hail, volcano and plague, sun and moon and stars are subject to His will; and through them He speaks to men. In earthquake, famine and plague, and all the catastrophes of the natural world we should hear God's trumpet calls warning us to repent and glorify Him.

With the blowing of the fifth trumpet we have the entrance of Satanic and demonic forces. (9:1-12.) The fallen star, the symbol of Satan, opens the pit of the abyss; and from this, as from Pandora's box, all forms of evil issue. The smoke which issues from the abyss shapes itself into the form of locusts—"demonic beings, like locusts in their form and flight, but like scorpions in their function." These symbolic creatures are grotesque and appalling because they are hellish in origin and nature. Their power is limited; for they are to torment only those who do not have the seal of God upon their foreheads. The fallen star that has the key to the bottomless pit is in contrast to "the bright and morning star," who has the keys of death and the grave. The 144,000 of 7:4 are the whole Church; all the saints of God are safe from the demonic powers. They have been marked with the seal of the divine ownership and protection. These hosts of Apollyon have power for five months—a brief, indefinite period, as God measures time. They are not to be identified with any particular person or period. There are writers who try to find an explanation for every detail of the symbolism, even to the tails and the hair and the faces of the dreadful locusts; but I have seen no particularized interpretation which is not a darkening of the picture by words without knowledge. It is better to take it as a picture of any short-lived, destroying force or evil influence in history, whose agents "thick as locusts, fearful as lions, intelligent as men, wily as women, malicious as scorpions, cause a state of misery and disorder in which death is preferable to life."[15] H. A. Taine, in his *The French Revolution*, says: "All the unfettered instincts that live in the lowest depths of the heart started from the abyss at once, not only the heinous instincts with their fangs, but likewise the foulest with their slaver." The trumpet of God's wrath and judgment did not sound for the first time in John's

[15] Baldinger, *Sermons on Revelation*. Used by permission of the author.

day, nor for the last in the French Revolution. Those trumpets were blowing over Europe in the second decade of our century; and they are sounding today.

The sixth trumpet (9:13-19) is followed by the loosing of the four angels that were bound at the river Euphrates; and the loosing of these angels of judgment is the preparation for a great invasion of hostile armies. The river Euphrates was the boundary, Israel's line of defense against her enemies. In the eighth chapter of Isaiah it is the symbol of the Assyrians. The loosing of the angels signifies that God's permission is given for the avenging hordes to rush in. God's restraint is removed, and destruction overflows the land. The terror-stricken imagination magnifies the physical characteristics of the inrushing hosts of evil. The whole description is marvelously magnified in harmony with the apocalyptic method. The four angels have been holding the forces of destruction in restraint; but now that restraint is removed, and the armies and horsemen of judgment and ruin come rushing in. The whole picture symbolizes the upheavals and terrors which preface the second coming of Christ; and brings us down again to the end of the Christian era. The effect of God's judgments is still the same. Men repent not of their works; they hold on to the things of the world—their idols of silver and gold, of brass and wood and stone. (9:20-21.)

But what is to become of the Church, of God's own people, in all the destruction and darkness, in this storm-swept welter of the world's ruin? "Behind the dim unknown, standeth God within the shadow, keeping watch above His own." And so we come over into the tenth and eleventh chapters and hear again the victory song: "The kingdom of the world is become the kingdom of our Lord, and of his Christ: and he shall reign for ever and ever." The section included in 10:1—11:14 comes between the sixth and seventh trumpets, just as chapter seven is placed between the sixth and the seventh seals. It gives to the Church the assurance of her safety in the upheavals that will accompany the impending judgments of God. John sees another strong angel coming down out of heaven; and his face was as the sun; and he had in his hand a little book open. (10:1-2.) This angel is Christ Himself, the Son of man seen by John in the first chapter; and the little open book is the gospel, the word of God for His Church. The angel lifts up His right hand to heaven and swears that there shall be delay no longer. (10:6.) The Christian age is drawing to a close, the final hour is about to strike. The mystery of God is to be finished. His whole purpose will be revealed, and men will no longer see through a glass darkly. That purpose which has been running through all the ages will be accomplished; and the fulfillment of that age-old purpose will issue in woe to those who reject Him and joy to those who follow His will.

John was about to write what he saw, but he heard a voice from heaven saying, "Seal up the things which the seven thunders uttered, and write them not." If all God's plan were revealed to man there would be no room for faith. There are some things in the eternal counsels of God which we may not now know. There are depths not yet fathomed. There are hidden mysteries in the purposes of God that cannot be revealed. "The secret things belong unto Jehovah our God," says Moses; "but the things that are revealed belong unto us and to our children for ever." (Deut. 29:29.) The little book does not answer all our questions. There are some things which must await the revealing light of eternity. But there is an "open book." It is a little book; and the content of this little open book is the message which John and his successors are to proclaim to many peoples and nations and tongues and kings. The Christian is always the colporteur of a book. This little book is to be eaten. Its contents are to be assimilated so as to know their value. And so the written word of God is not only to be read. It must be assimilated and absorbed and become a part of experience. The central substance of the little book's contents begins to be revealed in chapter twelve. In the meantime it is made clear that the little book is to be given to others. In the eleventh verse of chapter ten Christ's last great commission to His Church is expressed in symbolic form. The little book is to be given to other peoples and nations and tongues and kings.

In chapter eleven John comes again to the Church. In the measuring of the temple (11:1-2) we have the assurance of the Church's safety. It was measured for preservation. The temple referred to is not the temple in Jerusalem—that had been destroyed years before—but the temple of God's people, which, in Christ fitly framed together, groweth into a holy temple in the Lord—the household of God. (Eph. 2:19-22.) In the midst of destruction God's temple will be preserved from all peril. John is commanded to measure the temple and the altar and them that worship therein. The court without the inner temple is left outside and measured not. Those who trample the outer courts, who are only nominal Christians, are omitted from the measurement and from the security which the measurement symbolized. John draws a clear line of distinction between the true worshippers of God and those who mingle wickedness with their worship. "There is a ring of gold, a circle of protecting fire, around those who are truly Christ's." The unregenerate, the ungodly, the Gentiles, were to be allowed to tread the outer courts of the temple for forty and two months—for three and a half years, a short, indefinite period, yet covering the entire duration of the Church's history on the earth.

During this period when the Gentiles are trampling under foot the outer courts of the temple and the holy city, two witnesses bear testimony to the truth in the streets of the city. Here we have symbolized the continuity of the Church's witness in the world. There will always be those who witness for God's truth, clothed in sackcloth, "mourning for the corruptions against which they cry."

Those witnesses, all the true people of Christ, are immortal until their work is done. For twelve hundred and sixty days they testify—three and a half years.

This is the period during which the Gentiles are treading down the courts of the temple, the whole period of the Church militant's history. When they have finished their testimony, "the beast that cometh up out of the abyss shall . . . kill them." Their dead bodies are to be left lying in the streets, a mark of extreme indignity. The Jews buried the body on the day of death. In the *Iliad* fierce battles are fought for the possession of the bodies of the dead warriors. For three and a half days the bodies of the witnesses lie in the streets, while the world makes merry over their death. But after the three and a half days life reanimates the dead bodies of Christ's witnesses; and they stand upon their feet, their mission and their message vindicated. The world and the beast from the bottomless pit can never silence the voice of the Church. All through history there are illustrations of the fact that in the end the triumph of God's truth becomes evident.

> "Truth crushed to earth shall rise again,—
> The eternal years of God are hers;
> But Error, wounded, writhes in pain,
> And dies among her worshippers."

The world may kill the two witnesses of God's truth and in three and a half days many others will rise up to take their place and carry on their testimony. This is the dramatic story of the Church's witness, seen by John in all the "warmth of vision and prophecy."

After the episode of the measured temple and the two witnesses, the seventh trumpet is sounded and ushers in the end. The cause of Christ is finally triumphant, evil has been forever put down and the right is forever victorious. "The kingdom of the world is become the kingdom of our Lord, and of his Christ: and he shall reign for ever and ever." The kingdoms and empires of the world have succeeded one another and passed away; but His Kingdom is an everlasting Kingdom and His dominion shall not pass away.

The final issue of the Church's conflict is foreseen as

already realized. The four and twenty elders, the glorified Church, fall upon their faces and worship God. The time for the judgment of the dead has come, the time for the giving of rewards to the prophets and the saints, and to destroy them that destroy the earth. The work of the Redeemer is accomplished; God's purpose is fulfilled. The scepter of dominion over the world is at last wrested forever from the hand of Satan. Henceforth the world will know "holiness instead of sin, happiness instead of misery, life instead of death." There will be righteousness and peace and joy. This section of the vision is an unfolding of the future, a disclosure of things yet to be. The eye of the prophet sees into the distant future, and he is sure of the coming victory. We see only the advancing and retreating waves, the storm-tossed seas of today; and sometimes we grow discouraged. The seer on Patmos sees with "larger, other eyes than ours"; and he knows that

> "While the tired waves, vainly breaking,
>   Seem here no painful inch to gain,
> Far back through creeks and inlets making,
>   Comes silent, flooding in, the main.
> And not by eastern windows only,
>   When daylight comes, comes in the light;
> In front, the sun climbs slow, how slowly;
>   But westward, look, the land is bright!"

John heard the voice in heaven proclaiming that the kingdom of the world is become the kingdom of Christ. The powers of the world had arrayed themselves against Christ and His Church and had failed. In the final issue Christ is seen to be eternally victorious; and He shall reign for ever and ever. That was the revelation made to John. That was what made heaven ring with triumphant hallelujahs. That is the Christian conviction; that is faith's certainty—Christ is "the holiest among the mighty, and the mightiest among the holy, who with His pierced hands has lifted empires off their

hinges, turned the stream of centuries out of its chan-
nel, and still governs the ages." In the end

> "Jesus shall reign where'er the sun
>   Does his successive journeys run;
>   His kingdom stretch from shore to shore,
>   Till moons shall wax and wane no more."

As you gaze down the long dark road toward old age,
and the unknown world that lies beyond, never believe
that the road ends in darkness and oblivion; first the
evening and after that the morning. At the close of the
pilgrimage and all the warfare of earth the temple of
God is opened; and we see the ark of His covenant, the
symbol of His faithfulness and His love. The Church is
secure; she witnesses in a hostile world; she wins the
victory; and at the end through the open doors of
heaven she beholds the pledge of God's faithfulness in
the fulfillment of all His promises. (11:19.)

CHAPTER IV

THE FOURTH AND FIFTH VISIONS

1. THE FOURTH VISION: *The Radiant Woman, The Red Dragon, and His Two Beasts*

Revelation 12:1—14:20

THIS VISION carries us back to one of the most familiar verses in the Old Testament: "I will put enmity between thee and the woman, and between thy seed and her seed: he shall bruise thy head, and thou shalt bruise his heel." (Gen. 3:15.) In the vision John sees in symbolic form a holy war. He sets before us the figures of a woman, a man child, and a great red dragon. (12:1-6.) The meaning of these opening verses is clear: Christ is about to be born into the world; and over against this dawning power stands the dragon waiting to destroy the child as soon as he should be born. The child is caught out of his reach up to the throne of God; and the dragon turns to vent his baffled fury upon the faithful followers of the child.

The sun-clothed, star-crowned woman with child is the Church. She is clothed in light from head to foot. The sun, moon, and stars are the perfect emblems of light. Her child is the Son of Light. The woman is not to be identified exclusively with Israel, or the Old Testament Church. The Church of God is one, whether under the Old Testament or the New; and so here the woman symbolizes the Church in its widest meaning, the whole company of the redeemed. On earth, when measured by human standards, the Church appears as divided, with many faults and failures. Here, however, the vision revealed the ideal Church, viewed from the heavenly point of view, a glorious company of those

fulfilling the purposes of God. The eager and expectant
waiting of those devout souls who, before the coming
of Christ, were longing for the consolation of Israel is
fittingly symbolized here by the figure of an expectant
mother. There is also the suggestion that for the redemption of the race a new and divine force had to be
born into the world. There were in history, resident in
humanity, no forces sufficient to save the world. Salvation must come from God. "In the beginning was the
Word, and the Word was with God," but that Word
must become incarnate in human life in order to ac-
complish the will of God.

The dragon standing before the woman that he may
devour her child is Satan. He is great because of his
power, and the red color indicates the murderous fe-
rocity with which he destroys. The seven heads suggest
the completeness of his wisdom and cunning for the
execution of his plans. The ten horns are the symbol of
his power and of his rule over the kingdoms of the
world. This red dragon, the archenemy of the human
race, we meet in the first pages of Genesis; and we can
track the slime of his footprints through all the stages
of human history. Always his program is one of hate
and ruin and destruction. His standing before the expectant woman is a dramatic representation of the way
in which this embodiment of all evil seeks to destroy all
nascent good. Here he knows of the coming child to
whom the rule of the world had been given in the
counsel of God.

The man child, who is to rule all nations with a rod
of iron (12:5), is Christ, the promised Messiah. Satan
tries to destroy the Christ Child at His birth. Herod,
seeking to kill the Babe of Bethlehem, was acting as
the agent of the dragon, and manifesting satanic hate.
The Child, however, escapes the fury of the dragon: he
"was caught up unto God, and unto his throne." This
is the ascent of Jesus and His enthronement at the
right hand of the majesty on high, where He must
reign till He hath put all His enemies under His feet.
The vision passes over the entire earthly ministry of

Jesus, His crucifixion and resurrection, because the purpose here is simply to show that the dragon's power and craft and ferocious vigilance are futile.

The woman, the Church, having given birth to her child, "fled into the wilderness, where she hath a place prepared of God, that there they may nourish her a thousand two hundred and threescore days." (12:6.) Here again we have the symbolic three and a half years, the short and indefinite period as measured by the astronomical clock, which covers the whole history of the Church in the world. The wilderness life of the Church lasts during the whole of the Christian era. The wilderness represents an outward state of affliction, a state of separation from the visible presence of the Lord, the period intervening between the redemption wrought by Christ and His return to receive His Church and present her unto the Father a glorious Church, without fault or blemish or any such thing. In the meanwhile the Church is in the world, but not of the world, beyond the reach and power of her foe to hurt or destroy.

In verses seven to twelve of this chapter we have a picture of war in heaven and the casting out of the dragon. This portion of the vision may be retrospective; it may go back into the dim and distant past, and show how the dragon came to be on the stage of history, and the cause of the Church's conflict. Satan is a fallen angel. There had been war in heaven, and he and his followers had been defeated and cast out. (Jude 6.) The verses immediately following, however, seem to indicate that the reference is not to the original rebellion of Satan, but to new manifestations of his malice and power subsequent to the incarnation. This warfare the writer pictures in all the realism of the apocalyptic method. The dragon and his army were routed; and he and his angels were expelled from their former celestial place: "neither was their place found any more in heaven." Cast out from heaven, the Devil finds on earth a new stage on which he can carry on the conflict against God and all good. Woe comes

upon the earth because it is the battlefield; and the
wrath of the Devil is multiplied because he knows that
he has but a short time. The people of the Church overcome him because of the blood of the Lamb, and because of the word of their testimony; "and they
loved not their life even unto death." Here we have the
divine secret of the overcoming life: the fact of the
atonement of Christ on the cross of Calvary; and their
own open testimony to the word of divine revelation,
their faith in the saving power of Christ's death. Their
own faith and devotion to Christ were such that they
overcame the natural love of life. Their hope was built
on Christ, and in comparison with Him the world was
accounted as of nothing worth. "Their non-attachment
to life" was carried to the extent of being ready to die
for their faith. (12:11.)

In the remaining sections of this vision Satan tries to
destroy the Church: "he persecuted the woman that
brought forth the man child." The Church, however, is
not forsaken; she flees into the wilderness. For three
and a half years, during the whole of her militant history in the world, she is persecuted of Satan but pro-
tected and nourished of God. During this "short time"
her children experience the wrath of Satan. The world
is not their place of peace and rest. There is startling
boldness in the figure which represents the dragon as
casting out of his mouth after the woman a river of
water, "that he might cause her to be carried away by
the stream." (12:15.) To try to paint a picture of this
would be absurd. The writer is still appealing to our
imagination. His words are for "inspiration, not in-
formation." The attack upon the Church coming from
the mouth of the dragon is significant, indicating malicious accusation or destructive teaching. The Church in
history has ever been subject to calumny and flooded
by false doctrines. Many of the potent heresies of her
earlier days are remembered now only by historians of
dogma; and the present heresies will disappear as have
those of the past, swallowed up by the earth. We need
have no fear for the future of the Church. God who

has so marvelously kept her through the centuries that
are gone will keep her still until the "time, and times,
and half a time" be complete and she comes to glory.

> "See the gospel Church secure,
>   And founded on a rock!
>   All her promises are sure;
>   Her bulwarks who can shock?
>   Count her very precious shrine;
>   Tell, to after ages tell,
>   Fortified by power divine,
>   The Church can never fail."

Baffled in his attempt to destroy the woman, the
dragon went away to make war with the rest of her
seed (12:17); and he (not the "I" of the King James
Version) stood upon the sand of the sea (13:1). As
the red dragon stood there John saw a wild beast coming up out of the sea, coming at the call of his master.
This beast combines the fearful characteristics of the
four beasts in the vision of Daniel (7:3); he has the
ferocious courage of the lion, the dull brutishness of
the bear, the sudden swiftness of the leopard, and the
dreadful terribleness of the unclassifiable fourth creature. He bears also certain resemblances to the dragon,
for he has seven heads and ten horns, and on the horns
ten diadems. This beast is primarily the symbol of the
Roman world power by which the Church in John's
day was persecuted. In a wider sense it represents all
godless governments, empires, and political forces arrayed against Christ and His Church in any age. Rome,
this beast from the sea, is the agent of the dragon.
Rome, however, was only one representative of the
world power selected from one particular period of history, the period of the people to whom John was writing. The Devil is the Prince of the world; and the beast
in every age, from Babylon to Berlin, acts as his agent
and executes his evil will. John saw the people of the
world worshipping the dragon because he gave his authority unto the beast, "and they worshipped the

beast." The worship of the Roman emperor was just the question at issue when John wrote; for the Christians it was a choice between Caesar and Christ. Worship of the beast, the Devil's agent, is justified on the ground of his brute force: "Who is able to war with him?" (13:4.) It is the old philosophy of evil that might makes right. The fact is here clearly brought out that emperor worship, the worship of any state or nation or political power, is Devil worship. The beast from the sea has a mouth speaking great blasphemies, reminding us strikingly of some more modern powers, "and there was given to him authority to continue forty and two months"—three and a half years, the period of the Church's wilderness life, the period reaching down to the return of the Lord. Only those worship him whose names have not been "written from the foundation of the world in the book of life of the Lamb that hath been slain." (13:8.) For the Christians refusing to worship the emperor and opposing the power of Rome there was no hope for escape from suffering; but suffering would be the pathway to glory, and death the doorway into everlasting life. In the persecution and suffering from this godless, bestial world power there is need for all the patience and faith of the saints. (13:10.) As we read this portrayal by John we are reminded of items of news in our morning's paper.

John has also a vision of a second monster, the beast coming up out of the earth. He is spoken of as "another beast" (13:11); and he is the agent of the first beast, just as the latter is the direct agent of the Devil. This second beast represents, in the first instance, the native council of Asia Minor, the provincial government. The Roman central government was powerless to destroy the Church because of the intervening sea; and so it calls upon the beast from the earth, the local provincial power which acted as the executive of Rome. This beast has two horns like a lamb, but he speaks as a dragon. The function to which he devotes himself is religious. "He maketh the earth and them that dwell therein to worship the first beast." The two horns indicate the twofold function, civil and religious, which belonged to the Asian council. The care of the imperial cultus was one of the chief concerns of the native council; and so in verses fourteen and fifteen the asiarchs, or the local priests, employ magicians to work wonders and awe the minds of the people and compel them to the worship of Caesar. By magic they seek to subjugate the minds of the populace; and by the use of ventriloquism the image of the Roman emperor is made to give the advice that there be given to all a mark as an indication of loyalty to Rome. Emperor worship was the test; and boycott was one method of compulsion. Just what this mark was no one knows. Probably a certificate would be issued to those who submitted to the demands of the government. No follower of Christ could worship the beast and thereby comply with the conditions on which those certificates were issued. Before one could engage in trade, however, he must have that mark or certificate. No man who refuses the dominion of the godless world power may enjoy its privileges. That is as true today as it was in the days of John. And, therefore, these early Christians of Asia Minor were socially ostracized, and boycotted, and not allowed to buy and sell.

"Here is [need for] wisdom," says John. "He that hath understanding, let him count the number of the beast; for it is the number of a man: and his number is Six hundred and sixty and six." (13:18.) A pathetic loss of time and thought and mathematical ingenuity marks the labors of an endless list of men who have tried to solve the riddle of this mystic number and assign it to some particular person in history. It refers to no man; and at the same time it refers to every man who grasps political power and assumes religious prerogatives, and seeks to take the place of God as the Lord over the consciences of men. The number and not the name is the significant thing. It is a well-known fact that in Hebrew and in Greek the letters of the alphabet have a numerical value; and so any combination of letters could be expressed by numbers. A name could be spelled by the use of numbers. Many interpreters of Revelation believe that John used the number 666 to designate some historical person, whom he for obvious reasons could not mention in explicit terms. So far as we know the earliest attempt to interpret the number thus and refer it to a particular person was made by Irenaeus, in the second century, who thought that it spelled "Teitan," or Titan, and therefore meant a beast with Titanic power. He found also that the numbers in Greek letters add up to "Lateinos," which might be the true solution "because the Latins now bear the rule." From the days of Irenaeus on down to the present this mystic number has intrigued the minds of those who seek for a literal interpretation. About a century ago four German scholars discovered independently that this beast must have been the Roman emperor Nero. If you take the words "Nero Caesar," add the letter *n* to Nero, making it read "Neron Caesar," put the two words into Hebrew letters, and sum up the numerical value of these letters, you get the number 666. Others interpret the number as referring to Napoleon, the Roman Pope, the German Kaiser, Hitler, and various other historical characters whom they regard as personifications of sin. All such interpretations are confusion worse confounded. The number 666 is simply the symbol for triplicated evil—evil raised to the highest power. This beast to whom John assigns the sinister number represents the combination of malignant evil embodied in political power and false religious pretensions. The number is a symbol and not a cryptogram.

The name expresses the inner nature of the one to whom it is applied. The name of the Father expresses His character. The numerical symbol for the name Jesus in Greek is 888; and here the name of the beast expressed in numbers falls as far short of the perfect number 7 as the name of Jesus goes beyond it. To my mind, therefore, the number 666 refers to no particular man in history. The terrible, brutal beast, as seen and symbolized by John, stands for the wicked world

power, the power of gold and greed and cruel, bestial
selfishness, which is forever opposed to the spirit and
ideals of Christ. Here this beast has begun to assume
religious prerogatives and make religious claims, demanding the homage of men. "When the Devil steals
the livery of heaven, or when man steals the livery of
heaven in which to serve the Devil, you have the most
subtile and crafty form of evil." Its number is six
hundred and sixty and six. Only anti-Christian experience could know the name, the nature, of an anti-
Christ. Such experience no Christian could ever have.

The dragon, the first beast, and the second beast all
combined cannot avail to overcome the true followers
of the Lamb. In claiming the worship due to God alone
the world political power of John's day, and of every
other day, was putting itself on the side of the Devil,
and thereby sealing its inevitable doom. The effect produced upon the mind by the reading of chapters twelve
and thirteen is one of depression, discouragement, and
sorrow. But in chapter fourteen we have another con-
solatory vision, a parenthesis of hope and victory parallel to those disclosures made between the sixth and
seventh seals and between the sixth and seventh
trumpets. (Chs. 7 and 10:1—11:14.) This phase of
the vision reveals to the persecuted, suffering Church
the real issue of the conflict as God sees it. The Lamb
still stands upon Mount Zion and with Him are the
144,000, with His name and His Father's name written
on their foreheads. With the dragon is the beast and all
the world that worshipped the beast. But those that be
for us are more than those that be against us. Mount
Zion is the place where God dwells; and there is the
true throne of the universe. With the Lamb is the
whole company of the redeemed; and they sing a new
song which no man can learn but themselves. This
song was the expression of an experience through
which they had passed; and only those who had had
the experience could know and sing the song. The love
of Jesus, what it is, none but His loved ones know.

"Wouldst thou learn the ocean's secret?
In our galley thou must go."

In the first five verses of this chapter, as thus interpreted, John is looking again at the end of the age. He
sees the whole Church victorious and happy, and safe
in the everlasting kingdom of Christ. This is a vision of
comfort and encouragement to God's persecuted
people in all lands and in all ages. The meaning of the
vision is clear:

"Crowns and thrones may perish,
    Kingdoms rise and wane,
But the Church of Jesus
    Constant will remain."

In the following sections of this chapter we have
three angelic proclamations, and a voice from heaven
(14:6-13):

(1) Verses six and seven read: "And I saw another
angel flying in mid heaven, having an eternal gospel[16]
to proclaim unto them that dwell on the earth, and
unto every nation and tribe and tongue and people;
and he saith with a great voice, Fear God, and give
him glory; for the hour of his judgment is come: and
worship him that made the heaven and the earth and
sea and fountains of waters." The angel flying in mid
heaven is in the sight and hearing of all the universe.
The proclamation which he makes is not a final enunciation of the gospel message that the world at the last
moment may repent and be saved. It is the proclamation of the end, the second coming of the Lord, and
the judgment which that coming will bring. It is not the
gospel of salvation: it contains no call to believe in
Christ; no mention of mercy and forgiveness. It is not
the gospel of good news to all men; and it is proclaimed not unto but over them that sit upon the
earth.[17] The world hears the pronouncement of its

[16] A. S. V. Margin.
[17] See Greek text.

doom, the proclamation of the Judgment of God: "the hour of . . . judgment is come."

(2) The second angel proclaims the fall of Babylon. (14:8.) The mystic name Babylon is used to signify the seat of the world dominion, the seat of the first beast, the city of Rome. In I Peter 5:13, Babylon is used for Rome; and in the seventeenth and eighteenth chapters of Revelation, in the description of the godless city built on seven hills, we have convincing evidence that Rome is the place and the power here referred to. Rome in her pride and her licentiousness was a source of moral infection to the world. She is pictured here as the great harlot who has made all nations to become intoxicated and to commit fornication. Other pagan cities in history partake of the character of Babylon; and of all such Rome is a type. In whatever city the power of the world is worshipped, and the souls of men prostituted, there is Babylon. Any nation or political power in history that sets itself against the Kingdom of God is Babylon. The Rome of John's day had seduced the nations of the earth to the worship of the emperor, and now her doom had come.

(3) The third angel makes proclamation of the doom of those who worship the beast (14:9-12), and the blessedness of the holy dead (14:13). Here we have one of the most terrible pictures of the fate of the ungodly which Holy Scripture contains. Over against the torment of those who drink the wine of the wrath of God is set the felicity of those who die in the Lord. The images used in describing the torments of the lost are symbols, and do not lend themselves to literal interpretations. Symbols, however, express spiritual realities; and the realities are more than the symbols are able to express. When ordinary language fails man falls back upon the use of symbols in order more adequately to express the thing to be revealed; but always the symbol falls short of the reality. Over against the restlessness of those who have denied and rejected the Lamb, we have the patience of the saints, "they that keep the commandments of God, and the faith of

Jesus." (14:12.) In her refusal to submit to the cult of Caesar there was opportunity for the exercise of the Church's patience and endurance, as she kept the commandments of God and held fast to her faith in Christ.

Just before the manifestation of the Son of God in judgment we have that inexpressibly beautiful word from heaven with reference to the sainted dead: "And I heard a voice from heaven saying, Write, Blessed are the dead who die in the Lord from henceforth: yea, saith the Spirit, that they may rest from their labors; for their works follow with them." If the book of Revelation had done nothing more than give to bereaved and sorrowing men and women "this one perfect sentence, so noble in its comforting assurance, so incomparable in its lovely English," the value of this book to the Church would be beyond all human price. In the midst of the apocalyptic roar and storm of dreadful symbolism these heavenly words fall upon our ears like soft and subtle music. If you have ever stood by the bedside of a dying loved one, and, with bated breath and breaking heart, watched while the beloved soul took its flight, or if you have stood by the graveside and heard the cruel earth falling upon the casket to shut a dear face from view, you can understand something of the wonder of those words: "Blessed are the dead who die in the Lord."

This is one of the great—possibly the very greatest—of the many beatitudes of the Bible. It sums up in a single sentence the whole future of the blessed dead who have fallen asleep in Christ. They are forever free from all unrest and toil and poverty, and pain and weariness and sickness of the flesh. They are "without fault before the throne of God" (14:5, K.J.V.) and of the Lamb; and far away from the presence of sin. This verse does not reveal the future of all the dead, but only of the dead who die in the Lord. The voice from heaven is speaking only of those who die in the faith and the fear of the Lord Jesus Christ. The man or woman who would find the blessedness of those who die in the Lord must also live in the Lord in this world.

He or she, before the hour of death, must come to Christ in faith and say:

> "Just as I am, without one plea,
>   But that Thy blood was shed for me,
>   And that Thou bidd'st me come to Thee,
>   O Lamb of God, I come."

We Christians do not think as much about our beloved dead as we should. "Fear or false teaching about invocation of saints, and prayers for souls in purgatory, has made us Protestants almost forget what God has really told us about the dead." They are with the Lamb; and the nearer we draw to Christ the closer is the tie by which the living believers and the sainted dead are bound together. The Christian dead are at rest in the presence of God; and we are called to draw near to the same presence. We should think of our departed loved ones, who have died in Christ, as living, not as dead. Christ spoke to the dead as though they were alive and could hear, and they were alive and did hear; and came back at the call of His voice. No man is ever dead when his body lies lifeless. Those whom we have loved and lost for a while are absent from us; but we should think of them and love them none the less because of that absence. In the presence of God they are blessed, and in the keeping of God they are at rest. They rest from the toils, the pains, the problems, the sickness, the sorrows, the wrongs, and the weariness of the world. The most fitting way of announcing the departure of a good man is still the old-fashioned phrase: "He is at rest."

They rest from their labors, but their works follow with them to be continued and perfected in the other world. The rest of the life beyond does not mean inactivity; it does not mean idleness. God's people in the glory world "shall do Him service." Heaven is not a silent place, not a place of placid repose. Man is endowed with an endless capacity for work: he will want an occupation in heaven. Peace and companionship with God do not mean an Elysium for the drone and the sluggard. The Greek word that is translated labors carries the meaning of distressing, painful exertion, which involves fret and strain and exhaustion. In the saints' abode there will be work without pain and toil. Man's purified powers and faculties will be called into fuller exercise. "Their works do follow them"; and so the rest of the heavenly world is not the rest of sleep, nor of unconsciousness, nor of idle inaction. It is the rest of work from which all the element of painful labor and toil has been taken away. The works of heaven are one of the things that add to its blessedness. The labors of the saint's life end at death, but not his works.

The final section of chapter fourteen gives us a vision of the harvest and the vintage at the end of the world. Christ appears as the Son of man, at His second coming, on a white cloud; and in His hand He has a sharp sickle. (14:14-16.) The purpose of His coming is to reap the harvest of the earth, as is indicated by the sickle in His hand. The golden crown which He wears is the crown of royalty victorious, as He comes to conclude the story of the ages. "For the hour to reap is come; for the harvest of the earth is ripe. And he that sat on the cloud cast his sickle upon the earth; and the earth was reaped." This is only the harvest of the wheat—the servants of Christ who are reaped by the Son of man Himself.

The vintage of the wicked follows the gathering of the good. "And another angel came out from the temple which is in heaven, he also having a sharp sickle. And another angel came out from the altar, he that hath power over fire; and he called with a great voice to him that had the sharp sickle, saying, Send forth thy sharp sickle, and gather the clusters of the vine of the earth; for her grapes are fully ripe. And the angel cast his sickle into the earth, and gathered the vintage of the earth, and cast it into the winepress, the great winepress, of the wrath of God." The tares are gathered, as Christ gathered the wheat. The messengers of God's judgment gather the evil for their final doom. "And the winepress was trodden without the city, and there came out blood from the winepress, even unto the bridles of the horses, as far as a thousand and six hundred furlongs." The metaphor of the battlefield is here mixed with the metaphor of the winepress; but the apocalyptic writer is not bothered by the mixing of metaphors. The combination makes the representation all the more terrible. The horses of verse twenty are the horses upon which He that is Faithful and True, together with His enemies, rides forth to conquest. (19:14.) The thousand and six hundred furlongs clearly has a symbolic meaning. Four is the cosmic number, the number of the world. This is multiplied by itself and then multiplied by a hundred (ten times ten). The sixteen hundred furlongs, therefore, symbolize the whole surface of the earth. The judgment will be universal, reaching to every point of the compass. The figures of the symbolism are not to be calculated and the geographical areas are not to be measured. The writer simply uses this method to impress upon the imagination the terror of the judgment and the completeness with which all evil is crushed. This whole section is a symbolic representation of the final judgment when Christ comes to receive and reward His own, to destroy at last all His enemies; and to reign forever over a redeemed people. This representation of the end is in perfect harmony with that given by Christ Himself in Matthew 13:39-43.

And thus this vision, like each of the preceding, carries us over the whole course of the Church's history on earth; and brings us to the same glorious consummation. Using the events and personalities of the age in which he wrote, John gives us a condensed vision of the struggles and conflicts of the Church in all ages. This fourth vision opens with an account of the birth of Christ, and closes with a picture of His second coming at the end of the age. There is opposition, enmity, hatred, and conflict, but the Church passes through the centuries conquering and to conquer; and will finally

emerge from all her warfare completely victorious.
Even in one of the darkest hours of the world's history,
amid the persecutions and martyrdoms of the first
Christian century, we have the assurance that in the
end evil will be forever overthrown and good forever
triumphant—

> "For right is right, since God is God,
>   And right the day will win;
>   To doubt would be disloyalty,
>   To falter would be sin."

2. THE FIFTH VISION: *The Seven Bowls*
Revelation 15:1—19:10

IN THIS vision of the bowls we have another turn of
the kaleidoscope of the future, revealing to us under a
different aspect the same eternal principles of God's
government and leading to the same glorious issues.
This vision, like those preceding, covers the whole of
the Christian era, bringing us again down to the end. It
gives with a different stage setting the same drama of
the age-long conflict between the Church and the world
and the final issue. This section also shows clearly that
the Revelation is not written according to a plan of
chronological sequence. In chapter fourteen we have
just been brought down to the end, and seen the Son of
man upon the throne of judgment. We have seen there
the harvest of the righteous and the vintage of the
wicked. We would naturally expect this to be followed
by the revelation of the new heaven and the new earth,
and the glory of the perfected reign of Christ. Beginning with chapter fifteen, however, the writer takes us
again over the weary course of history, showing again
the eternal principles of God's government; His judgments upon sin; and the ultimate issue.

The vision of the bowls bears a close resemblance to
that of the trumpets. There is, however, a significant
difference. The trumpets are warnings and the judgments are incomplete. In the case of the bowls the

judgments are intensified and consummated. The series
of judgments here symbolically portrayed does not begin until chapter sixteen. The fifteenth chapter is introductory. In the visions of the seals and the trumpets,
the parenthesis of comfort and consolation comes at
the close. Here, in the vision of the bowls, the chorus
of comfort and encouragement comes at the beginning,
before the judgments fall. A song of thanksgiving
preceded the opening of the seven-sealed book (5:9-
14); and a silence and offering of incense came just
before the blowing of the trumpets. And so in the fifth
vision, immediately after seeing the seven angels, having seven plagues in which is finished the wrath of
God, John saw "as it were a glassy sea[18] mingled with
fire; and them that come off victorious from the beast,
and from his image, and from the number of his name,
standing by the glassy sea,[19] having harps of God. And
they sing the song of Moses the servant of God, and
the song of the Lamb, saying, Great and marvellous
are thy works, O Lord God, the Almighty; righteous
and true are thy ways, thou King of the ages. Who
shall not fear, O Lord, and glorify thy name? for thou
only art holy; for all the nations shall come and worship before thee." (15:2-4.) This song of the saints in
glory precedes the pouring out of the bowls of God's
wrath. They stand by the crystal sea of heaven, a sea
of peace and calm, and sing the song of Moses, "I will
sing unto Jehovah, for he hath triumphed gloriously"
(Ex. 15:1); and the song of the Lamb, "Unto him that
loveth us, and washed[20] us from our sins by his blood;
and ... made us to be a kingdom, to be priests unto
his God and Father; to him be the glory and the dominion for ever and ever" (1:5). Those who sing have
come up from the fiery seas of the world's persecutions
to the shores of the heavenly sea. The song of Moses
commemorating the divine deliverance of Israel from
Egypt was sung by the Israelites at the hour of the eve-

[18] A. S. V. Margin.
[19] A. S. V. Margin.
[20] A. S. V. Margin.

ning sacrifice. Here, by the glassy sea, the Church has
passed through an experience of redemption greater
than that experienced by ancient Israel at the Red Sea;
and so the old song is recast and the sense of deliverance and victory deepened. The symbolism of the
glassy sea and the victorious singing saints may have
been suggested to John as he looked out across the
waters of the Aegean to the sun setting in the west. In
his "mystic state" he is standing by a sea of glass
mingled with fire. Anyone who has seen the radiant
colors of sunset reflected on the waters of a calm and
peaceful sea can appreciate the beauty of the picture.
On the shore of the sea is gathered a company of victorious and joyful singers, who have fought themselves
free of the beast and his image and the number of his
name. "They have the conqueror's abiding character."
They see their Pilot face to face, by the crystal sea:

> "By God's will
> Doubt not, the last word is still
> Victory."

Over against the reward of the righteous is placed
the wages of sin. (15:5-8.) The temple of heaven is
opened, and out of it—from the immediate presence of
God—come the seven angels that have the seven
plagues. Their clothing denotes the purity and beauty
of holiness; and the golden girdles about their breasts
are suggestive of affection, fidelity, and readiness to
serve. Their work is pointed out to them by one of the
four living creatures, representatives of redeemed
creation. We must go back to chapter four for the symbolism of these living creatures. As Milligan puts it:
"All creation owns the propriety of the judgments now
to be fulfilled."[21] "One of the four living creatures gave
unto the seven angels seven golden bowls full of the
wrath of God." (15:7.) The laws and forces of nature
fill the bowls of wrath and place them in the hands of

[21] *The Book of Revelation* (in the *Expositor's Bible* series).

the avenging angels. The plagues which follow the pouring out of the bowls are the penalties of broken laws, "the toll that nature collects from her disobedient children." The bowls are seven, indicating the perfection, the completeness, of God's wrath. When the bowls have been delivered to the angels nothing remains but to pour them out. The moment is one of terror, and the awful suspense of it is pictured in verse eight. The hour of judgment has come, the day of repentance is past, the night of doom has fallen; and no one can enter the temple. The smoke that fills it is the symbol of the majesty and holiness of God, and of the smoldering fire of His wrath against sin. Our God is a consuming fire. None could enter into His presence, no prayer could avail to avert the impending punishment; but when the seven plagues of the seven angels are past, the smoke will disappear, and the clear vision of God be seen.

In chapter sixteen the seven angels pour out the bowls of God's wrath upon the earth. As already indicated, the plagues which follow the pouring out of the bowls are similar to those which followed the blowing of the trumpets; and yet they are different in purpose and in extent. The trumpets were calls to repentance, the bowls are the visitations of wrath in punishment. The trumpet judgments were partial, extending only over a third part; the judgments of the bowls are final and complete. In the case of the bowls, judgment falls upon men from the very first, whereas the trumpet judgments do not reach them until the sounding of the fifth trumpet.

John heard a great voice out of the temple, saying to the seven angels, "Go ye, and pour out the seven bowls of the wrath of God into the earth." (16:1.) These symbolic bowls are reminiscent of Jeremiah's cup of the Lord's righteous wrath. (Jer. 25:15.) They represent the judgments and woes of God upon the wickedness of the world. The first bowl is poured upon the land and becomes a noisome and grievous sore upon the men that bear the mark of the beast and that worship his image. The imagery is drawn from the sixth plague in Egypt. The land, upon which this plague is poured, is the dwelling place of the second beast, political power claiming religious prerogatives. The punishment of the Roman Empire and its agents, the persecutor of God's people and the exponent of idolatry, is what the writer has in mind all the way through this section.

The second bowl is poured upon the sea, the place of the first beast, the seat of ungodly government; and the sea became as "blood ... of a dead man"; and every living thing in the sea died. The third bowl is poured into the rivers and the fountains of the waters, and it became blood. The echoing of the Egyptian plagues is clear. The rivers and the fountains are the feeders of the sea, and the blasting of God falls upon the sources of godless government. The waters are personified and, through the voice of their angel, confess the righteousness of God's judgments upon those who poured out the blood of saints and prophets. The justice of the judgment is proclaimed by those upon whom the judgment falls; and the altar, on which are the prayers of the saints (8:3), and under which are the souls of the martyrs (6:9), makes an antiphonal confession of the justice of God's judgments (16:7).

The fourth bowl, like the fourth trumpet, affects the sun, and the sun which should be a blessing becomes a curse, scorching men with great heat. The moral effect of the visitation is not remedial. Instead of repenting, men blaspheme the name of God who has brought suffering upon them. The wickedness of the worshippers of the beast is only intensified by their punishment, and their rebellion finds expression in words of blasphemy. (16:9.) When the conscience of man has been seared and deadened by deliberate and persistent sin there is nothing softening or converting in the judgments of God. A man may willfully silence the voice of conscience and push her restraining hands away, and pursue his evil course in utter defiance of the will of God; and the time will come when the voice of conscience will be silent. The heart may become so hardened that even the torture of the burning sun of divine wrath cannot burn into it the saving fear of God which leads to repentance and confession of guilt. "Sin is a curse, which, if left to run too long, can never be cured."

With the pouring of the fifth bowl we pass from the sphere of nature over into the spiritual realm, the place of the rulers of the darkness of this world, the realm of the beast. (16:10-11.) The bowl is poured upon the throne of the beast, and his kingdom is darkened. The earlier judgments have fallen upon the subjects of the beast; but now the very seat of his dominion is assailed; and the whole empire is covered with a thick pall of darkness which is the harbinger of impending doom. There is more than darkness, for the effects of the earlier plagues continue. They gnawed their tongues from the pain of the burning sun, and the malignant sores. Each bowl adds new punishment to those which precede; the punishment and consequent suffering are cumulative. The whole kingdom of evil is engulfed in blackness and torments. It was never the purpose of the writer of the Revelation that his figures and symbols should have specific application to particular characters and events in history. For a commentary on these woes, however, one might well read Gibbon's *The Decline and Fall of the Roman Empire;* or Carlyle's *The French Revolution;* or any authentic current history of affairs in Russia, Italy, Germany, or Spain. All over the world today there are men and women and little children who know what it is to gnaw their tongues in the agony of the woes which are come upon them, as the awful pall of darkness and doom settles over the kingdom of the beast.

Again, as in the case of the fourth plague, "they repented not of their works." Their tongues are gnawed in pain and frenzied rage; but they utter no prayer of penitence, they speak no plea for forgiveness. Torments do not cure men of their wickedness nor cleanse them from sin. They may in the hardness of their impenitence be driven into deeper sin and fouler blasphemies. Men may rebel against God and all goodness until the very spirit of evil settles in upon their souls and there is no hope for them. John gives us a graphic and awesome picture of the effect of God's judgments upon those who persistently reject His message of love and refuse to accept His precious rule. Today we do not emphasize as much as we should the fate of those who do defiance to the will of God. We have not deeply realized ourselves, and therefore we do not make others realize, that a man's sins will find him out and that the wages of sin is death. Sin and judgment and punishment are inevitably bound together. Even the incense bowls of the heavenly altar are full of the wrath of the holy God for those who despise and neglect His offered salvation. "Angels of the heavenly temple stand girt in gold prepared and ready to pour them out."

The sixth bowl, like the sixth trumpet, carries us to the river Euphrates. As far back as the memory of man could reach, this great river had run its winding course, stretching away for a distance of eighteen hundred miles. It was the natural barrier which held back the enemies of Israel. Now the sixth bowl is poured out upon this mighty river, and its waters are smitten and dried up. The kings from the sunrising find an easy passage when they come as messengers and agents of the wrath of God. The barrier which restrained is removed. Who these kings from the East (16:12) are nobody knows, and conjecture is profitless. The apocalyptic writer has in mind the judgment of God upon the persecuting power of Rome; but when any nation rots in its heart and dies in its soul, God always has prepared and held in reserve some other nation or nations ready to come in and crush her. "She ultimately becomes food for carrion beasts and birds of prey."

Verses thirteen and fourteen picture the hosts of evil against which these kings of the East, the agents of God, go into battle and gain the victory. Out of the mouth of the dragon, and out of the mouth of the beast, and out of the mouth of the false prophet (i.e.,

the beast from the land of chapter 13:11-18) come
unclean spirits in the shape of frogs. They are spirits of
demons, working signs; which go forth unto the kings
of the whole world, to gather them together unto the
war of the great day of God, the Almighty. (16:14.)
The great day of God which is here spoken of is primarily the day of decisive conflict between the worship
of Caesar and the worship of Christ. The frogs are the
offspring of the Devil, the godless government, and the
false religion; and they stir up and incite the enemies of
God to attempt to abolish the government of God from
the earth. They came from the mouths of the dragon,
the beast, and the false prophet, suggesting thus the
thought that the chief means of their influence is en-
ticing speech. "They are frog-like in that they come out
of the pestiferous quagmire of the universe, do their
devilish work amid the world's evening shadows, and
creep and croak, and defile, and fill the ears of the nations with their noisy demonstrations, till they set all
the kings and armies of the whole earth in enthusiastic
commotion for the final crushing out of the Lamb and
all His powers." Before the last great conflict between
the forces of good and the forces of evil these spirits of
hell go forth to persuade and seduce and deceive and
stir up the nations and governments and kings of the
earth to unite in an expedition which shall prove to be
the most disastrous expedition ever undertaken by
man. In verse fourteen we see this grand army of the
Devil's republic gathering together for the great conflict; and in verse fifteen the seer hears the voice of the
Captain of Salvation: "Behold, I come as a thief."
Unannounced and suddenly He comes to the rescue
and deliverance of His own, and they are to be watch-
ful and waiting.

In verse sixteen we stand at Armageddon, the place
where the final battle is to be fought. The evil spirits
gathered their hosts together into the place which is
called in Hebrew Har-Magedon. On the plain of Es-
draelon stood Megiddo. This place was made famous
by two great slaughters—that of Canaanitish hosts by

Barak, which was celebrated in the song of Deborah (Judges 5), and that in which King Josiah fell in the battle with Pharaoh-necho (II Chron. 35:22). The low hills around Megiddo have witnessed "perhaps a greater number of bloody encounters than have ever stained a like area of the world's surface." There was, therefore, a peculiar fitness in the choice of this name as the place of the last great struggle between the powers of good and the forces of evil. Of course the name is symbolic. The Armageddon of the Revelation has no location on the geographical map of the world. The place of Armageddon is nowhere, and it is everywhere. That battlefield is the world; and it is also within the soul of man. Some of us may be today in the midst of our Armageddon. The field of battle is also world-wide; and the warfare has been in progress for centuries. In the purpose of God and under the power of God it moves toward a final climax and culmination. In the course of the conflict nations rise up against nations and kingdoms against kingdoms. The kings of the earth set themselves and the rulers take counsel together against the Lord and against His anointed. Through the years there are wars and rumors of wars; there are famines and pestilences and earthquakes. All these things are but incidents in the great warfare which goes on from age to age; and which will continue until the complete triumph of truth over error, of good over evil, of light over darkness. John in vision sees the culmination of the conflict and calls it Armageddon. The battle of Armageddon, however, is not one in which physical armaments will decide the issue. That battle will be ended when Christ comes in victory and forever manifests His right and power to reign.

The seventh and last bowl is poured upon the air, the special sphere of Satan, the prince of the power of the air. Thus the seventh bowl with its blasting of the realm of Satan brings us on to the end. Evil now receives its final blow in the very center of Satan's dominion. With the emptying of the seventh bowl a voice

from heaven proclaims, "It is done." (16:17.) God's
purpose is fulfilled: the kingdom of the world is become the kingdom of our Lord and of His Christ. First
there is the voice, making proclamation of the fulfilled
purpose; and then there is the shaking of the heavens
and the earth with such an earthquake "as was not
since there were men upon the earth." Some of the effects of the earthquake are mentioned. (16:19-21.)
"The great city was divided into three parts, and the
cities of the nations fell: and Babylon the great was
remembered in the sight of God, to give unto her the
cup of the wine of the fierceness of his wrath." "The
great city" is Rome and Babylon is Rome; and Rome
is the symbol of all concentrated godless world power.
This judgment of God, however, is no local visitation—everywhere the cities of the nations are shaken
into ruins. John here is portraying eternal principles,
not definite historical events. The inevitable and terrible judgment of God upon sin is the great fact revealed—

> "Day of anger, day of wonder!
> When the earth shall rend asunder,
> Smote with hail, with fire, and thunder."

As in the former visitations, there is again no repentance and no conversion. "Men blasphemed God because of the plague of the hail; for the plague thereof is
exceeding great." Those who suffer and blaspheme are
the determined followers of the beast. They have the
very spirit of Antichrist, and so they sin and curse and
blaspheme to the bitter end, "unchanged and un-
softened by all the terribleness of an oncoming perdition." They do not curse their sins and their folly but
they curse God for disturbing their peace and their
pleasures. Their actions are suggestive of a Dance in
the Chamber of Death, and remind us of Bartholomew
Dowling's poetic description of a time of famine and
plague in India:

"There's a mist on the glass congealing,
  'Tis the hurricane's fiery breath;
  And thus does the warmth of feeling
  Turn ice in the grasp of death.
  Ho! stand to your glasses, steady;
  For a moment the vapor flies:
  A cup to the dead already,
  Hurrah for the next who dies!"

So much importance is attached to Rome, the center of the persecuting power of John's day, that two whole chapters (17-18) are devoted to the portrayal of her doom. These two chapters are in the nature of an episode, enlarging in greater detail upon the fate of Rome, which has already been foreshadowed in 14:8 and 16:19. The sun-clothed and star-crowned woman of the twelfth chapter is the symbol of the Church. The scarlet woman of the seventeenth chapter, riding upon the scarlet beast, symbolizes the corrupt and idolatrous power of pagan Rome. This adulterous woman of false religion is the source and center of the moral iniquity and deadly influence of the age. She is the mother of abominations. The scarlet beast upon which she rides is political Rome, the sea-born beast of the thirteenth chapter. This beast is an organized power, a godless world empire built on might. In John's day that beast was political Rome. In Luther's day it was the union of political and ecclesiastical Rome. In our own day the scarlet beast is mirrored in any one of several great world powers that one might mention, in which is embodied and manifested the world's hostility against the cause of Christ. "The worst is ever the degradation of the best"; and so John, carried away by one of the angels of the seven bowls, sees a woman. She was arrayed in purple and scarlet, denoting her splendor and luxury. The gold and precious stones and pearls suggest her material wealth and magnificence. In her hand she carried "a golden cup full of abominations, even the unclean things of her fornication"——her customs of idolatry and the tyranny with which she enforced her blasphemous claims upon the homage of men. Upon the forehead of the woman is written a name: *Mystery, Babylon the Great, the Mother of the Harlots and of the Abominations of the Earth.* The name has a symbolic meaning, and in verse seven the angel says, "I will tell thee the mystery of the woman," I will explain the symbolism. In the explanation that follows it is made clear that the beast is the anti-Christian empire of Rome, and he is "to go into perdition." The seven heads of the beast are seven mountains on which the woman sitteth; they are the seven hills on which the city of Rome was built. The seven heads are also interpreted as seven kings (verse 10)—"the five are fallen, the one is, the other is not yet come; and when he cometh, he must continue a little while." It is possible that these seven mountains, which are seven kings, are to be interpreted as the manifestation of the beast in successive periods of persecution and oppression through which the people of God have passed. Egypt, Assyria, Babylonia, Persia, and Greece have been suggested as the first five: and they "are fallen." Rome would, therefore, be the sixth; and it "is" in John's day. The seventh was to arise in some subsequent era. For an appreciation of the meaning of the Revelation for our day, however, it is better to forget the seven heads and ten horns in all save the symbolic sense, and remember that the great fact to be represented is that any nation or empire, any king or kingdom, which sets itself in opposition to the plan and purpose of God, and persecutes the people of God, will ultimately go down in ruins.

The scarlet woman is the city of pagan Rome. The beast upon which she rides is the imperial power, the empire. There have been in history many influential persons and powers strikingly similar to those which John sets forth under the symbolism of the repulsive woman riding upon the terrible beast. This section in the book of Revelation simply gives us a highly dramatic and symbolic portrayal of movements and principles, "of great historic forces and tendencies that were asserting themselves in John's day and in Rome's day, and have continued to operate every day since. You will find the seventeenth chapter of Revelation not only illustrated but fulfilled, again and again, wherever in history a false, apostate religion has sat astride a corrupt political power, holding the bridle reins of civil government and riding roughshod over all opposition toward its worldly goal."[22] In John's day the harlot woman of emperor worship sat astride the scarlet beast of Roman political power, and set out to exterminate the little group who were followers of Christ, and rode to utter and inevitable failure and ruin. At a later day the scarlet woman of Islam climbed upon a beast of civil government, and with the scimitar of war sought to destroy Christendom. We find illustrations of the same thing when the harlot woman of Romanism rode upon the scarlet beast of civil power, and became drunk with the blood of the saints and martyrs of Jesus. In the days of the Puritans in England, the Huguenots in France, and the Covenanters in Scotland we see again the scarlet woman riding upon the scarlet beast. We have seen it in Germany and in Japan. Whenever religion and politics become confederate, it means ruin for religion and for the state also. If in our American civilization we ever have a state-ridden church or a church-ridden state, we shall witness the crumbling of the very foundations upon which our nation and our Church are built. "Whenever a Church forgets her high office of spiritual supremacy and begins to covet worldly power and to reach forth her hand to the control of government, ... that Church is turning down a road at the other end of which is a woman in scarlet sitting astride a scarlet beast."[23]

John is never in doubt about the final issue of the coalition between religious and political power for the persecution of God's Church; and so in chapter eighteen we have a graphic representation of the utter

[22] Baldinger, *Sermons on Revelation*.
[23] Baldinger, *Sermons on Revelation*.

destruction of Babylon, the end of Rome as a material city and as a spiritual symbol. Everything that opposes the kingdom of Christ—the organization, the state, the institution, that sets itself against God—will go down in ruins. Only one city, Rome, is selected as an illustration of this fact. The causes of her fall are given with striking clarity in verses seven to seventeen: She glorified herself, she built on material values, she made commerce of slaves and trafficked with the souls of men. Rome in that day was politically and commercially supreme and her voluptuousness enriched the merchants of the earth. The world laments her fall, kings and merchants and sailors all unite in the mourning. Her fall involves others in ruin. Over against the dirge voiced by all those whose power, position, wealth, and livelihood perished with the destruction of Rome, there rises a psalm of joy and triumph from the saints, apostles, and prophets, whose prayers find fulfillment in the downfall of the persecuting power. "Rejoice over her, thou heaven, and ye saints, and ye apostles, and ye prophets; for God hath judged your judgment on her." (18:20.)

So great is the guilt of Babylon, so disastrous is her fate and so complete her destruction, that in the closing paragraph of chapter eighteen John dwells upon it from a different point of view. In a concise, graphic, and dramatic way he shows us the effects of the destruction when in one sudden hour the city is plunged into complete ruin. "The voice of harpers and minstrels and flute-players and trumpeters shall be heard no more at all in thee"; all the joy and gaiety of life as expressed in song and music is taken away. "And no craftsman, of whatsoever craft, shall be found any more at all in thee; and the voice of a mill shall be heard no more at all in thee"; the shops are closed, the shuttles and other instruments of industry and activities of production cease, and there is no longer the cheerful sound of the millstones which tell of food being prepared within the homes. The lamps are dark in the houses and upon the streets, and "the voice of the

bridegroom and of the bride shall be heard no more at
all in thee"; marriage ceases and there is no provision
for the continuance of life in new generations. The
destruction is complete. Babylon is destroyed; "and in
her was found the blood of prophets and of saints, and
of all that have been slain upon the earth." (18:24.)
The curtain falls upon the city "deep in ruin as in
guilt," and again the drama draws to the end. God is
on the side of His people, and He will never forget His
promises, nor will His faithfulness fail. A godless and
guilty world in the end feels the terror of His avenging
and destroying wrath.

The first ten verses of chapter nineteen are to be
linked with the closing verses of the eighteenth chapter.
They belong in the fifth vision; and in them we have
the hallelujah chorus of the saints set over against the
lamentations of the kings and merchants and sailors.
The saints who here sing are not exclusively the saints
in the heaven beyond the grave. They are in the realm
of the righteous, whether in the world of time or eternity. The whole ransomed Church of God praises Him
because He has inflicted upon the harlot the just punishment for her sins. The redeemed of Christ never sing
over the sufferings of humanity, but they do rejoice and
praise God for the triumph of righteousness and truth.
It is a heartbreaking thing to hear the wails and lamentations of kings, and merchants and shipping men, and
scarlet women, and traffickers in souls and bodies. It is
a heartbreaking thing to think of ruined cities, whose
streets are filled with the silence of death, and in which
no light of lamp sends out its friendly gleam to pierce
the gloom of the overshadowing blackness. It would be
a far more heartbreaking thing if godless nations and
men and women were allowed to travel unchallenged
and unhindered the criminal paths of harlotry and cru-
elty and greed and degeneracy, and manifest unhindered every form of wicked rebellion against the righteous will of God.

When John closes his fifth vision with a great throng
singing, "Hallelujah; Salvation, and glory, and power,

belong to our God: for true and righteous are his judgments," they were rejoicing, not over the doom of the sufferers, but because truth and righteousness were triumphant, and evil was overthrown. Their hallelujahs re-echo in "The Battle Hymn of the Republic"—

> "Mine eyes have seen the glory of the coming of the Lord:
> He is trampling out the vintage where the grapes of wrath are stored;
> He hath loosed the fateful lightning of His terrible swift sword:
> His truth is marching on."

This vision closes (19:6-10) with the marriage supper of the Lamb. The Church, the Bride of the Lamb, has been prepared through all the storms and conflicts of history; she has washed her robes and made them white; she has waited for Him, crying over and over again, "Come quickly." Now He comes and the eternal union is consummated. The marriage supper is celebrated and the Church shall be forever with her Lord. As the glory of the future opens before the writer's view the heavenly messenger bids him write: "Blessed are they that are bidden to the marriage supper of the Lamb." And the fifth vision closes with the words, "Worship God: for the testimony of Jesus is the spirit of prophecy." In Him all God's revelation centers. He is the manifestation of the God whom no man had seen. All true prophecy bears witness to Him, who is the beginning and the end, "over all, God blessed for ever."

CHAPTER V

THE SIXTH AND SEVENTH VISIONS

1. THE SIXTH VISION: *The Word of God Victorious*

Revelation 19:11—20:15

IN INTERPRETING the visions of the Revelation we should constantly divest our minds of the idea of succession in time. Each of the visions covers the whole period of history between the two comings of Christ; and there is no suggestion of temporal succession of the one after the other. Each vision is a revelation of the same principles of God's government, and of the same central idea of ultimate victory which is the dominant motive of the whole book. John employs the method of recapitulation. Each of the visions goes over the same interadventual period. Each rises above the other in a climactic spiral. This sixth vision is the climax, and in it all of the emphasis is placed upon the triumph of Christ's Kingdom. Throughout these lectures we have repeatedly emphasized this fact because an appreciation of it is necessary to the understanding of the book as a whole. In the preceding visions the judgments of God upon the rebellious powers and opposing forces of the world and His protection and deliverance of His own have been set before us in various aspects. The sixth vision brings us to a climactic conclusion, showing again that back of all history is the supreme will and work of the conquering Word of God. In the fifth vision the bowls parallel the trumpets of the third vision; and so also the sixth vision corresponds to the second. The two are linked together by the rider on the white horse, who is the Word of God going forth conquering and to conquer.

112

In the second vision the judgment was potential; in the sixth vision judgment is completely enthroned and the powers of evil are forever destroyed.

The vision opens with the appearance of a white horse, and he that sat thereon called Faithful and True; and as the vision unfolds we see the victory of the Word and the overthrow of every power that opposes His Kingdom. This is not a representation of the visible second coming of Christ. The white horse is the same figure that appeared with the opening of the first seal; and we are carried back again to the first advent. The description of the rider makes clear who He is. He is faithful; no word of His shall fail. He is true: He is real, essentially one with God. The living and victorious Word of God rides forth, with the sharp two-edged sword of speech issuing from His mouth, to the final triumph of the gospel of salvation. His eyes are like a flame of fire, penetrating and piercing so that no enemy will escape His vision. On His head are many diadems, which are symbolical of the universality of His sovereignty. He is called Faithful and True; but there is also an ineffable name of mysterious significance, "which no one knoweth but he himself." However much of His divine nature may be made manifest, there are always depths which no man can fathom. No man knoweth the Son save the Father. He is panoplied for war and the armies of the heavenly host accompany Him. These celestial troops are, like their Leader, mounted on white horses. The Word of God fights, not with carnal weapons, but with the word proceeding out of His mouth—the sword of the Spirit, which is the word of God. With the sword of His word He searches out the hearts of individuals and of nations and "cuts to the center of civilizations." On His garment and on His thigh there is another name written: "King of Kings, and Lord of Lords." He is to smite the nations and rule them with a rod of iron. He treads the winepress of the fierceness of the wrath of Almighty God, which has already been referred to in 14:19-20.

"From victory unto victory
His army shall He lead,
Till every foe is vanquished,
And Christ is Lord indeed."

John shows us the Conqueror riding forth to conflict: the Son of God goes forth to war. The action
moves swiftly to a close, for the dominating idea is that
of the complete and final victory. And so John carries
us across the intervening centuries of history and shows
us in symbol the ultimate issue. To him the triumph of
the cause of Christ is so certain that he does not tell us
how the warfare will end. He speaks of it as already
ended. He does not ask us to wait for the revelation of
the slow-moving centuries as they come and go. With
the wings of prophetic vision he leaps across the ages
and stands upon the border of the last age. There he
sees the birds bidden to gather at the great supper of
God's vengeance. They are to feast upon the flesh of all
the enemies of the Lamb. The slaughtered hosts of
God's foes become a meal for all the foul and ravenous
birds of carrion. The picture of the prophet Ezekiel
(39:17-20) is undoubtedly in the seer's mind; but
there is also a striking contrast with the joyful banquet
at which the children of God celebrate the marriage of
the Lamb to His Bride. "Blessed are they that are bidden to the marriage supper of the Lamb"; and over
against this the angel standing in the fiery sun cries:
"Come and be gathered together unto the great supper
of God." All humanity will be present at one or the
other of these two suppers. Those who accept the invitation to the marriage supper of the Lamb will enter
into the eternal City of God. Those who reject that invitation will go finally to the great supper of God's
judgment.

The battle of the centuries is not seen, but the call to
all the birds of heaven to come to the great feast suggests the completeness of the victory—the final
destruction of Caesar worship and of all the enemies of
the Church. It is a graphic, symbolic picture of a com-

plete conquest, an absolute victory. It is a portrayal of the perfect triumph of the Son of God over all the forces of wickedness. Not by any literal war, but by the preaching of the gospel is the victory won. To sum up what we have been saying, what John discloses to us here is not the second coming of the Lord, but a picture of the conquering career of the gospel of Christ in the world; and of the gospel's ultimate victory. In the last three verses of chapter nineteen the punishment proceeds. The warfare has come to a conclusion and the victory has been won. The beast was taken, and with him the false prophet; and "they two were cast alive into the lake of fire that burneth with brimstone." The beast and the false prophet are not persons, but personifications. The beast is the same as heretofore (e.g., ch. 17), the representation of the anti-Christian world in all its forms and forces. The false prophet is the second beast of chapter thirteen. (13:14.) The two are always associated—godless governments and false religions. They are cast into the lake of fire that burneth with brimstone, the place of eternal punishment. The fact of hell is clearly taught, but the imagery is not to be taken literally. The language is symbolic; but here also the symbol falls short of the reality. The lesson here is plain. Rebellion against God ends in death of the deepest kind. No weapon uplifted against the King of Kings can prevail. Those who will not have Christ to rule over them must perish. The sword of the King of Kings and Lord of Lords is mightier than all the powers of wickedness, mightier than all the forces of earth and hell combined. Those who neglect His mercy, despise His love, and stand out against His righteous rule will eternally die.

In chapter twenty John continues his theme: Victory. There are three great enemies of Christ and His Church—the dragon, the beast, and the false prophet. In chapter nineteen the beast and the false prophet have perished; but the dragon, the Devil, remains. His destruction is reserved for the end. The ultimate enemy back of the beast and the false prophet is Satan. The overthrow of Satan, not a fancied reign of a thousand years over some geographical Utopia, is the theme of the first ten verses of chapter twenty. Here is a symbolic setting forth of the end of the conflict and the final victory over the last great enemy. We should approach this chapter with great humility of spirit, recognizing its difficulties, avoiding dogmatic statements, and respecting the honest interpretations of others. This chapter has been spoken of as the "fighting chapter" of the Bible. It has been a bitter debating ground for Christians who are fond of controversy and who hold irreconcilably different views of its meaning. Your interpretation of this chapter will determine whether you take your stand with the pre-millenarians, or the post-millenarians, or the non-millenarians. John, in his visions on the isle of Patmos, never dreamed that his readers would debate and divide over the contents of this chapter.

As we try to interpret chapter twenty—following our method of not combating rival interpretations but of following John Calvin and stating simply the true meaning—let us bear in mind that the book of Revelation is an apocalypse, produced in a time of persecution, characterized by the use of symbolic and highly figurative language. It was intended to comfort and encourage people who were passing through a period of great trial and affliction. It had a meaning and a message for the readers of the day in which it was written. The twentieth chapter is in method and purpose in complete harmony with the rest of the book. In our Bibles there are 66 books; 1189 chapters; 31,173 verses. Nowhere else in all these books and chapters and verses does the idea of a millennium occur. Only in the twentieth chapter of Revelation, verses two, three, four, five, six, and seven, do we find this mystic word. If verses four, five, and six had been omitted from this chapter no one would have dreamed of a literal thousand years of Christ's reign on earth; of His setting up a temporal throne in Jerusalem and inaugurating a millennial reign as an earthly monarch. To build an entire system of eschatology and a philosophy of history on these three highly figurative verses is a precarious thing to do. Due regard for the symbolism of numbers solves here the problem of interpretation; and harmonizes the teaching of this chapter with all the remainder of the Word of God.

This twentieth chapter of Revelation falls naturally into four divisions:

(1) The Binding of Satan, verses 1-3.
(2) The Souls of Martyrs and Confessors Enthroned with Christ, verses 4-6.
(3) The Final Battle between Satan and the Saints, verses 7-10.
(4) The General Resurrection and the Final Judgment, verses 11-15.

The resurrection, the last judgment, and the second death follow the second coming of Christ; and there is no period of years in between. All Christians are agreed as to the great fact of Christ's second coming. The teaching of it in the Bible cannot be eliminated or explained away. The Christian faith and hope centers around the fourfold revelation concerning the incarnation, the atonement, the present advocacy, and the future advent of Jesus Christ. In our celebration of the sacrament of the Lord's Supper we bear unchanging testimony to the Christian conviction concerning our Lord's promised return: "For as often as ye eat this bread, and drink this cup, ye do shew the Lord's death *till he come*."[24] Christian faith looks with grateful adoration back to the cross; and it looks forward also with eager expectancy to the coming of the Christ who died on the cross and rose again. Christ *has* come. He has entered as the ultimate factor in human history. He will come again in the glory of the Father with His angels and judge every man according to his works. Much of the powerlessness and lack of passion in the Church to-

[24] I Corinthians 11:26, King James Version.

day are due to the neglect of this cardinal element in the Christian creed. Imaginative speculations, the fixing of dates, the drawing of charts, and unscriptural interpretations of the plain teachings of the Bible have done much to discredit this blessed hope in the minds of practical men and women, who try to live with their feet on the ground. Other important doctrines of the Bible, however, have suffered in the same way at the hands of their friends.

If the Word of God be taken as our final authority, then the fact of the second coming of Christ is beyond all room for debate. Our hope for the ultimate and eternal reign of righteousness and peace and gladness rests not on purely human power and policies. The golden age of humanity in its final phase will be ushered in not by our schemes for social reconstruction, not by political powers, nor international alliances; but by the promised coming of Christ. And so we look upward and forward, believing that the grace of God hath appeared, bringing salvation to all men; and "looking for the blessed hope and appearing of the glory of the great God and our Saviour Jesus Christ; who gave himself for us, that he might redeem us from all iniquity." (Titus 2:13-14.) This is the faith of the Church through the ages. "He ascended into heaven, and sitteth on the right hand of God the Father almighty; from thence He shall come to judge the quick and the dead." "This same Jesus, which is taken up from you into heaven, shall so come in like manner as ye have seen him go into heaven." (Acts 1:11.)[25]

It is said that the New Testament contains 380 references to this promised visible return of Christ. We are taught to be faithful in the Christian life and work because "yet a little while, and he that shall come will come, and will not tarry." (Heb. 10:37.)[26] The last book in the Bible opens with the prophecy, "Behold, he cometh with the clouds" (1:7); and ends with the

[25] King James Version.
[26] King James Version.

promise, "Yea: I come quickly," and the prayer, "Even so, come, Lord Jesus" (22:20).[27] This revelation of the second coming of Christ was given not for the satisfaction of speculative curiosity, but as an incentive to Christian faith and hope and love, and for the comfort of longing, aspiring, and sorrowing human hearts. In meditating upon this fact of Revelation we should first of all divest our minds of all the wild vagaries of many modern adventists cults, and of millennial dawnism in its various forms. The visible return of Christ is not the foundation stone of Christian faith. It is only one among several great elements in the Church's creed.

> "Living He loved me, dying He saved me,
>   Buried He carried my sins far away,
>   Risen He justifies, freely forever,
>   One day He's coming—oh, glorious day!"

Christ's spiritual presence with His faithful followers is a fact of present experience: "I am with you always." There are also repeated comings of Christ mentioned in Scripture and experienced in life. He came in the presence and power of the Holy Spirit at Pentecost. He came in the destruction of Jerusalem by the Romans in A.D. 70. He comes into the heart of the Christian at the hour of conversion; and He comes to release him in the moment of death. But there is in addition to all these a promised *"parousia"* of the Lord, a future, visible, glorious appearing. This future appearing is called "the second coming of Christ" to distinguish it from the great first coming at the time of the incarnation and manifestation in the days of His flesh. This second coming will be with power and great glory to deliver His faithful followers forever from the power and the presence of sin, to raise the dead, to institute the final judgment, and to inaugurate the final phase of His messianic kingdom.

The book of Revelation, in harmony with the con-

27 King James Version.

sistent teaching of Christ and the New Testament writers, dwells upon the thought of the gradual triumph of Christianity in individual lives, in human institutions and society. The good is increasingly triumphant over evil; but the completion of the history awaits the coming of Christ. The Kingdom of God comes as a developing process; but the process culminates in a catastrophic coming. In the course of human history the Church in each generation is a witnessing Church, a missionary agency. In proportion as the Church is true to her mission the principles of Christ become more and more operative in human society and civilization. The number of Christian individuals and groups will increase. The Church will ever be the medium through which the light of the world shines out upon and enlightens the darkness of the world. As the Church witnesses and works she also waits and watches for the coming of the Lord.

The world, however, will not be completely Christianized by the work of the Church and by the preaching of the gospel. The conflict between the good and the evil will continue until the end of the age. The disciples of Christ are commissioned to preach the gospel in all the world for a witness unto all nations; but they are not promised that all the world will be converted by their preaching. They themselves will be hated and despised and persecuted even until the end. Wars shall continue, all the results of evil will be manifest, there will be no lasting peace preceding the *parousia*. There shall be tribulations and trials and distress down to the end; and there shall be the falling away of many. The golden age of the world, the ideal society, will never be the result of purely evolutionary forces, nor the product of human plans and policies. The holy city, the New Jerusalem, comes down from God. And so at the end of the age Christ will come in power and great glory for the completion of the conquest of the good over the evil. Then will be the general resurrection and the great judgment. Then will the world see—

"The Judge that comes in mercy,
    The Judge that comes with might,
    To terminate the evil,
    To diadem the right."

This is the consistent teaching of Scripture and this is
the continued faith of the Church as embodied in her
great historic creeds. Chiliasm, millenarianism, or pre-
millenarianism in its simple form goes back to the early
days of the Church. It originated very largely in Jewish
apocalyptic hopes; but has been held by many sincere
and scholarly interpreters of sacred Scripture. It has a
legitimate place in the history of Christian doctrine and
should not be classified as an heretical teaching. Post-
millennialism originated in the first quarter of the
eighteenth century with the teachings of one Daniel
Whitby (d. 1726). Post-millennialists hold to the theory of a millennial period in history, an age of gold and
glory; but they believe that this period will precede the
second coming of Christ. According to their view the
millennium is a thousand years' period of the spiritual
reign of Christ on earth, when the world shall have
been completely converted to the Christian religion,
and all human relations will be in harmony with the
principles of Christ. The second advent will come after
this period, hence the name "post-millenarian" from
the Latin preposition *post,* meaning after. From the
time of Whitby, millenarians began to speak of themselves as "premillenarians," from the Latin word *pre,*
meaning before; and thus indicating that they expect
the second advent to come before the millennium. In
the second quarter of the nineteenth century an ex-
clergyman of the Church of England, John Nelson
Darby (1800-1882), founder of the Plymouth Breth-
ren, developed the doctrine of dispensationalism. According to his peculiar theory the Old Testament saints
and those to be saved during the supposed period of
the Church's history on the earth after the second advent, do not belong to the Church, the Bride of Christ.
Christ came and offered the Kingdom to the Jews; the

offer was rejected and then withdrawn. Christ did not
set up His Kingdom at His first coming, but postponed
it. We are now living in the Church age, and there is
no such thing as the Kingdom of Christ on earth today.
The Gospels of the New Testament (especially the
Synoptic Gospels) are not for the Church, but for the
postponed kingdom which is to be set up in visible and
material form, with Jerusalem as its capital, when
Christ comes to establish His millennial reign. The true
Israel of God has no continuity in the Christian
Church; and we Christians may not with propriety pray
"the Lord's Prayer." "It is one of the rags which Luther brought away from the old Roman sepulchre."[28]
The present Church period is a parenthesis in history
to which the Old Testament prophets make no reference.

As we have said above, simple millenarianism
should not be looked upon as heresy; for it has had "the
right of citizenship in the Christian Church" from the
very early days of the Church's history. If, however, we
define heresy as "doctrine that contradicts the historical
universal Christian faith," or as "an opinion opposed
to the commonly received doctrine, and tending to
division or dissension," then Darbyism, or Dispensationalism, as it is widely taught today is heresy—
hurtful in its influence and hindering to the work of the
Church as a divine institution for the advancement of
the Kingdom of God. It has no legitimate place in the
Reformed faith, for the Westminster Confession of
Faith enthrones Christ as "executing the office of King,
in subduing us unto Himself, in ruling and defending
us, and in restraining all His and our enemies." Christ
is now "head over all things to the church, which is his
body, the fulness of him that filleth all in all." (Eph.
1:22-23.) In his book, *What Is The Kingdom of God?*
Dr. R. C. Reed reminds us that the demons could not

[28] A. C. Gaebelein, *The Gospel of Matthew*. Used by permission of the author.

enter the herd of swine, "could not even hurt a hog without permission of Jesus."

Let us return to the fourfold division of chapter twenty given above; and seek to interpret the teaching of the chapter in the light of what we have just been saying and in harmony with the whole of God's revelation. Scripture must be interpreted by Scripture; and isolated proof texts, taken apart from their native setting, should not be made the basis of new systems of doctrine.

1. In verses 1-3 we have the binding of Satan: "And I saw an angel coming down out of heaven, having the key of the abyss and a great chain in his hand. And he laid hold on the dragon, the old serpent, which is the Devil and Satan, and bound him for a thousand years, and cast him into the abyss, and shut it, and sealed it over him, that he should deceive the nations no more, until the thousand years should be finished: after this he must be loosed for a little time." John here is giving us not a statement of literal fact, but a portrayal of spiritual truth expressed in symbolic form. The angel did not have a material chain, and a spirit cannot be literally bound. The thousand years does not mean a literal period in history of one thousand times three hundred and sixty-five days. To give so literal an interpretation to so symbolic a passage is to do violence to all sound principles of Scriptural interpretation. The angel with the key and the great chain in his hand stands for Christ Himself. If the expression "a thousand years" be given any definite temporal content, its *terminus a quo* would of necessity be the binding of Satan. When was Satan bound? In Mark 3:27 (Matt. 12:29) Christ says: "No one can enter into the house of the strong man, and spoil his goods, except he first bind the strong man; and then he will spoil his house." In these words we have a distinct allusion to the binding of Satan, and at the same time a clear intimation of the meaning of the passage before us. Again Christ said to His disciples: "I beheld Satan fallen as lightning from heaven." (Luke 10:18.) Just before His

death, on the occasion of the visit of the Greeks, Jesus said: "Now is the judgment of this world: now shall the prince of this world be cast out." (John 12:31.) In His farewell discourse with His disciples, on the night before His death, He said to them, "The prince of this world hath been judged." These words of Jesus all have reference to what John speaks of as the binding of Satan. With the triumphant death of Christ upon the cross the Devil, in all his dominions, received a blow from which he will never recover. In the narrative of the temptation of Jesus in the wilderness we have the beginning of the binding of Satan. That binding was completed in the work of the cross. There Satan was bound, but not destroyed. We see his end when he is cast into the lake of fire and brimstone for ever and ever. (Rev. 20:10.) The thousand year expression simply means the perfection or completeness of his binding. It has no definite temporal significance; and yet, of course, there is a temporal period over which the binding extends. This period reaches from the death of Christ on the cross of Calvary to the time of His second advent. It is the whole period of the Christian dispensation, the period of the Church militant and her conflicts in the world. During this period Satan is completely bound, he is deprived of his power as over against the saints of God. And he cannot prevent the heralding of the gospel to all nations. He will make war against the believers, cast the righteous into prison, persecute and kill them; but their true life is beyond his reach, they are hid with Christ in God. He is still, however, the ruler of the world, the deceiver of the wicked, the prince of the powers of darkness.

The apparent difficulty in verse three is the expression "that he should deceive the nations no more." This difficulty disappears, however, if we place the emphasis on the pronoun *he*—"that *he* should deceive the nations no more." By the work of Christ on the cross Satan was completely bound; and yet the Devil's work is still carried on in the world. That work is done for him, as Weymouth suggests, "with inferior power and skill and diminished success by subordinate evil spirits." These are the principalities and powers and world rulers of this darkness, and the spiritual hosts of wickedness in heavenly places of which Paul speaks, and with whom is our warfare. Verses 13:14 and 19:20 tell us who are now the deceivers of nations. These are the agents of the Devil and sufficiently account for the ungodliness and wickedness of the world. They have sufficient force and cunning to deceive the nations without the personal presence and activity of Satan. Dr. B. B. Warfield thinks it quite possible that the binding of Satan and his loosing are contemporaneous events. In this case the thousand years and the "little time" are concurrent, in so far as any time element is concerned, and cover the whole period down to the end of the present era. For the saints on earth this period is "a little time," a broken time, three and a half years. For the saints in glory it is "a long and blessed period passing slowly and peacefully by, while they reign with Christ and enjoy the blessedness of holy communion with Him—'a thousand years.'" During this period Satan is bound: he cannot hurt the saints of God, neither can he prevent the establishment of Christ's Kingdom among the nations of the world. Our own conviction is that the "little time" of verse three is the period covered by the events of verses seven to ten, when Satan is again permitted to gather his hosts and the fire from heaven destroys them—at the close of this age. As the age in which we are living draws near to the end there will be an intensifying of the forces of evil. The opposition to the Church and its work will be world-wide; and the powers of paganism and all ungodliness will combine in a concerted effort to overcome the Kingdom of Christ. For "a little time" Satan will be loosed.

2. In verses four to six we have a vision of the martyrs and confessors enthroned with Christ. John says: "And I saw thrones, and they sat upon them, and judgment was given unto them: and I saw the souls of them that had been beheaded for the testimony of

Jesus, and for the word of God ... and they lived, and
reigned with Christ a thousand years. ... This is the
first resurrection. Blessed and holy is he that hath part
in the first resurrection: over these the second death
hath no power; but they shall be priests of God and of
Christ, and shall reign with him a thousand years." No
other passage in the Bible has given rise to more controversy than this; and yet as a matter of simple fact it
is of little practical importance save for those how
make it the basis for millenarian systems of thought.
As indicated above, apart from these verses in the
twentieth chapter of Revelation, not only the term
"millennium" but the idea itself is unknown in the
Christian Scriptures. The reigning of the saints with
Christ for a thousand years is simply the positive side
of the binding of Satan. John knows nothing of their
reigning in an earthly kingdom. The message of this
passage is the message already given to us in the words
of 14:13: "Blessed are the dead who die in the Lord
from henceforth." The reigning of the saints with
Christ for a thousand years is a reigning in heaven,
away from "the confused noise and garments bathed in
blood that characterize the war upon earth." The reign
is located in the spirit world and not on earth. What is
meant by this symbolic and beautiful description of
"the holy peace of Christ's saints is not the fore-
shadowing of a period in the earthly history of the
Church, either before or after the second advent; but
for a far more profound and practical revelation of the
intermediate state of the righteous dead,—the bliss of
Christ's people safe penned in Paradise." "The millennium of the Apocalypse is the blessedness of the saints
who have gone away from the body to be at home with
the Lord."[29] The thrones which John saw are thrones
in heaven, not on earth. Those who sit upon the
thrones live and reign with Christ for a thousand years;
they have come into a state of perfect and glorious vic-

---

[29] Warfield, *Biblical Doctrines.* Used by permission of Oxford University Press, publishers.

tory and rest. The thousand years symbolize the idea of perfection, but again the time element is not wholly excluded. The period of the reigning of the saints is the entire interadventual period. This period covers many centuries of human history, but it is not an endless period. It will come to a close, so far as time is concerned, at the second coming of Christ, when these souls now reigning with Christ in glory will be united with their resurrection bodies. "The rest of the dead lived not until the thousand years should be finished." From the time of their death until the coming of Christ and the final judgment they were apart from God and from Christ. Their names were not in the book of life—they "lived not." "He that hath not the Son of God hath not ... life." (I John 5:12.) Thus with reference to the rest of the dead, the wicked dead who had died without peace with God, John preserves a holy reticence. He simply contrasts their intermediate state with that of the righteous dead by saying that they "lived not." They are dead in the deepest sense of that word, suffering now the penalty of sin and rebellion against God; and in the end they shall be plunged into the terrible "second death" of the lake of fire. (Vs. 14.) At the coming of Christ they, as well as the souls of the godly, will receive their bodies and pass into their eternal state. This is the uniform testimony of Scripture.

"The first resurrection" of verse five is not regeneration. These martyrs and confessors were already regenerate before they partook of the first resurrection. Their bodies had died, but their souls, released from the dying bodies, had ascended into the glory of heaven. The first resurrection is also not a bodily resurrection. John says plainly, "I saw the souls of them that had been beheaded." There is no warrant in the Word of God for belief in two bodily resurrections, one of the righteous and one of the wicked, separated by a thousand years of time. The New Testament elsewhere always brings the second coming of Christ and the general resurrection and general judgment into close chronological connection. It nowhere places a long period between the resurrection of believers and unbelievers. It teaches only one bodily resurrection, and that one is at the time of the second coming of Christ. Jesus plainly teaches that the resurrection of believers takes place at the last day. (John 6:39, 40, 44.) The ascension of the redeemed into heaven is the first resurrection. This fact of the first resurrection is beautifully expressed in the words of the Westminster Catechism: "The souls of believers are at their death made perfect in holiness, and do immediately pass into glory; and their bodies, being still united to Christ, do rest in their graves till the resurrection." That statement is an exposition of the saints living and reigning with Christ for a thousand years, that is the first resurrection. Over those who have a part in this first resurrection the second death, the lake of fire (vs. 14), has no power. In the eighth verse of chapter twenty-one the second death is fully explained as eternal punishment in the lake of fire and brimstone.

3. In verses seven to ten there is a representation of the final battle between Satan and the saints: "And when the thousand years are finished [i.e., when the Christian era comes to a close], Satan shall be loosed out of his prison, and shall come forth to deceive the nations which are in the four corners of the earth, Gog and Magog, to gather them together to the war ... And they went up over the breadth of the earth, and compassed the camp of the saints about, and the beloved city." So long as human nature remains the same there will be danger of new outbreaks of evil "from the bottomless pits of human passion." The dragon is unchained, Satan is released from his prison for "a little time," and again allies himself with some great world force. The new forces of evil that will in the latter days appear and encompass the Church, John symbolizes by the gathering together of innumerable hosts from the four corners of the earth. "Out of the regions beyond the fringe of the Roman Empire vague barbarian forces from the confines of the world" shall

mass themselves and move across the stage of history in a new conflict against Christ and His Church. Gog and Magog of verse eight are names that appear in Ezekiel, chapters 38 and 39. Gog is a prince and Magog is the land over which he rules. In Jewish apocalyptic literature the names became symbolic of the enemies of Israel, which were to be overthrown in the Messianic age. Here they represent the last great uprising against the dominion of Christ. There is no possibility of identifying them with definite historical figures. They are personifications of the last enemies of the Church, and their uprising will be the final assault of the world against the cause of Christ. They gather the forces of evil together for war, as the frogs do with the kings in 16:14 (their number "is as the sands of the sea"); the conflicts of the future would be even more severe than those of John's day. The "camp of the saints" is the Church of Christ; and "the beloved city" is the same Church, the body of Christ represented as a community under the protecting care and love of God. In contemporary history there is much that is suggestive of this loosing of Satan and his final assault upon the saints and the "beloved city"; but Christ warns us against trying to fix the times or seasons which the Father hath appointed.

The mustering of the forces of evil here portrayed is Satan's last and desperate effort to thwart the will of God and destroy the Church. This effort also fails; for "fire came down out of heaven, and devoured them." (Vs. 9.) In this descending fire we have symbolized the second coming of Christ, coming to rescue and reward His faithful servants and to forever destroy all His and their enemies. "Our God is a consuming fire." And here we have "the revelation of the Lord Jesus from heaven with the angels of his power in flaming fire, rendering vengeance to them that know not God, and to them that obey not the gospel of our Lord Jesus: who shall suffer . . . eternal destruction from the face of the Lord and from the glory of his might, when he shall come to be glorified in his saints . . . in that day." (II Thess. 1:7-10.) Christ comes, "and the devil that deceived them was cast into the lake of fire and brimstone, where are also the beast and the false prophet; and they shall be tormented day and night for ever and ever." This is the end of Satan. All his cunning has been frustrated, his power broken, his forces destroyed; and now his doom is forever sealed. From the lake of fire there is no release. This, looked at from the negative side, is the one far-off divine event to which the whole creation moves. After the gospel of the Kingdom shall have been preached in the whole world for a testimony unto all the nations, then shall come the end. (Matt. 24:14.)

4. Finally, in verses eleven to fifteen, we have the general resurrection and the final judgment. After all the millenniums of history Christ shall come, the dead shall be raised, the issues of human life shall be summed up, and judgment shall be passed upon all. John saw "a great white throne, and him that sat upon it . . . And . . . the dead, the great and the small, standing before the throne; and books were opened: and another book was opened, which is the book of life: and the dead were judged out of the things which were written in the books, according to their works." In the end Christ appears in person, leads His Church in her final victory, destroys her enemies, and sits upon the throne of His judgment. The judgment is to be universal: all of the dead stand before Him; and the books, which contain the records of the lives of all, are opened. Millions of men and women have lived and died of whom the world knew nothing; their names appear on no earthly documents, but the records of all are written in heaven. This is John's symbolic representation of the divine omniscience.

Verse thirteen re-emphasizes the universality of the judgment: "And the sea gave up the dead that were in it; and death and Hades gave up the dead that were in them: and they were judged every man according to their works." There have been many shipwrecks and many bodies lost at sea, and many have been buried there where no gravestones could mark their resting places; but in the end the sea will give up its dead. The entire realm of death and Hades shall be emptied and all shall be judged. The impressive thing in chapter twenty, for us the most practical thing, is this great judgment and opening of the books. We have here one of the most solemn and compelling passages in the whole Bible. The throne is great in comparison with all other thrones; and its whiteness is suggestive of the stainless purity of Him who sits upon it. Before this throne people of every land and every age, and of every nation and kindred and tribe and tongue, are assembled to receive the holy Judge's verdict. We must all appear before the judgment seat of Christ, that every one may receive the things done in his body. (II Cor. 5:10.) The standard or basis of judgment is "according to their works"—things thought, things spoken, things done. This is a just basis of judgment. It is according to nature; and nature never forgets. The day of reckoning may be postponed, but in the end as a man soweth so also shall he reap: the books are opened. But there is another book, the book of life; and this contains the names of those who in this world have found their portion in Christ. After the other books have been opened, the book of life is opened. In it are the names of those who have washed their robes and made them white in the blood of the Lamb. By the record of the other books there could be nothing but condemnation; but there is no condemnation for them who are in Christ and whose names are found in the book of life. Martin Luther in one of his night visions saw the Devil come into his room with great volumes of books which he commanded the monk to read; and he saw in his dream that these books contained the record of his life, and that they were written with his own hand. The Devil said to him, "Is that true? Did you write it?" The poor terrified monk had to confess that the record was true, and that his hand had written it all. When the Devil had reduced the stricken man to hopeless misery, he picked up his books and turned to go; but at that moment another vision came to Luther, and he cried to the Devil and said: "It is true, every word of it; and my hand wrote it; but across it all write, 'The blood of Jesus Christ cleanseth us from all sin.' " The works by which the Christian will be judged are his faith and trust in Christ.

This method of interpreting the twentieth chapter of Revelation recognizes the apocalyptic character of the book, is in harmony with sound principles of exegesis, and does no violence to the plain meaning of other passages in the Word of God. According to the consistent teaching of Scripture and the faith of the Church, as embodied in her historic creeds, there is a future age of gold and glory. This age of righteousness and peace, however, this perfect kingdom of God, will not come until Satan with all his forces and followers has been forever overthrown. John, in his vision, sees an era of blessedness, when sin and sorrow and suffering and death shall be done away. That era he describes not by the limited term of a thousand years, but by the beautiful picture of a new heaven and a new earth; and that picture is found not in chapter twenty, but in chapter twenty-one. The second coming of Christ precedes and inaugurates this golden age. Peace and righteousness and joy shall some day characterize this very earth on which we dwell. When John speaks of a *new* heaven and a *new* earth he uses the Greek word for *new* which designates something that already existed but now appears in a new aspect. He is not speaking, therefore, of a heaven and earth which shall for the first time come into existence, but of an already existent heaven and earth which are now transformed. John sees the earth as it shall be when the Church shall have accomplished her mission, when the Kingdom of God shall have fully come, when His will shall be perfectly done on earth as it is in heaven, when Christ shall have come, and Paradise shall have been regained. Then the prophecies of Isaiah 2:4 and 11:6 shall be realized. After the return of Christ there will be the restoration of all things. The whole creation which now groaneth and travaileth in pain will then be renewed and glorified. In the closing chapter of Second Peter, the writer declares that "the day of the Lord will come ... and the earth and the works that are therein shall be *discovered*" (A.S.V. margin; not "burned up"). Peter there predicts the world transformation and not the destruction of our present physical world. The issue of Christ's coming will be a new and better world wherein dwelleth righteousness. Thus interpreting the twentieth chapter of Revelation, we are in harmony with the other teachings of God's Word on this great subject; and we can unite in the prayer:

> "Come, and make all things new;
> Build up this ruined earth;
> Restore our faded Paradise,
> Creation's second birth,
> Come and begin Thy reign
> Of everlasting peace;
> Come, take Thy Kingdom to Thyself,
> Great King of Righteousness."

To the interpretation of this section of Revelation as thus outlined, objections may be found. We believe that there are greater objections to any other exposition of this difficult passage. Whatever system of interpretation we may adopt, it should be presented without dogmatic assurance. The central thought of the writer in this passage is the final and utter failure of Satan; the complete and eternal triumph of the cause of Christ. This triumph will come with the fulfillment of that "blessed hope and appearing of the glory of our great God and Saviour Jesus Christ." (Titus 2:13, margin.) In the interpretation of the details of John's splendid vision Christians may differ; but the essential thing, the coming of Christ and the victory of His cause, is a part of the common faith once for all delivered unto the saints.

2. THE SEVENTH VISION: *The New Jerusalem*

Revelation 21:1—22:5

IN THIS closing vision we have set before us the Church Triumphant, perfected, glorified, and the new heaven and the new earth that follow. This last vision of Revelation is not an idealistic portrayal of the Church as she now is, but a realistic picture of the Church as she will be. The ideals of the present become the realities of the future. Here we have the final issue of the conflict; and here we pass from time into eternity. Here we have Paradise Regained, the true "Millennium," the age of glory and of gold. To this millennium, which lies beyond the coming of Christ, there is no end. The enemies of the Lamb of God have all been completely conquered and destroyed; the great day of judgment is over; the old order of things has passed away. John sees the bliss and glory of the heavenly world, in which the redeemed shall forever dwell with Christ. He sees the eternal home which Christ has prepared for His own, for those who in faithfulness have followed Him during their earthly pilgrimage, who have "climbed the steep ascent of heaven through peril, toil, and pain." Their struggles and their conflicts on the field of history issue in a new heaven and a new earth. The followers of other religions find their golden age in the past: for the Christian this era of perfection and of bliss is one which the future yet holds in store—"new heavens and a new earth, wherein dwelleth righteousness" (II Peter 3:13); the regeneration when the Son of man shall sit on the throne of His glory (Matt. 19:28); "the times of restoration of all things, whereof God spake by the mouth of his holy prophets that have been from of old" (Acts 3:19-21). In this section, then, we have the unveiling of that which the Apostle Paul speaks of in I Corinthians 2:9-10: "Things which eye saw not, and ear heard not, and which entered not into the heart of man, whatso-

ever things God prepared for them that love him. But
unto us God revealed them through the Spirit: for the
Spirit searcheth all things, yea, the deep things of
God."

First John sees a new heaven and a new earth. As
indicated already, the word "new" that is here used
does not mean that the heaven and the earth which
John saw are now for the first time brought into being.
They are the old heaven and the old earth, but they
are transformed, they have "a new aspect, a new character, adapted to a new end." The old will die and a
new will issue from its tomb. The new heaven and the
new earth correspond to the new man whose renewal
has now been perfected in the restoration of all things.
Here we have the fulfillment of the promise in Isaiah
65:17, "Behold, I create new heavens and a new earth;
and the former things shall not be remembered, nor
come into mind"; and 66:22, "the new heavens and
the new earth, which I will make, shall remain before
me, saith the Lord." War and pestilence and famine
are left behind; the dragon, the beast, and the false
prophet have met their fate in the lake of fire; Armageddon is ended; the eternal separation has been
made; the Lamb of God is forever triumphant.

The beauty and wonder of John's words fall upon
our ears like soft and entrancing music from some
faraway glory world: "I saw a new heaven and a new
earth: for the first heaven and the first earth are passed
away; and the sea is no more. And I saw the holy city,
new Jerusalem, coming down out of heaven from God,
made ready as a bride adorned for her husband. And I
heard a great voice out of the throne saying, Behold,
the tabernacle of God is with men, and he shall dwell
with them, and they shall be his peoples, and God himself shall be with them, and be their God: and he shall
wipe away every tear from their eyes; and death shall
be no more; neither shall there be mourning, nor crying, nor pain, any more: the first things are passed
away." (21:1-4.) These words were not written for the
mechanically minded. When we are told that there

shall be no more sea, of course the words are intended to be interpreted symbolically; for there could be no fruitful and beautiful earth without the sea. The sea is the symbol of separation, of isolation, and of unrest. The sea represents the stormy and turbulent realm out of which the terrible persecuting beast rose. The sea was the thing that shut John off and separated him from his beloved fellow Christians who so much needed his shepherding care. It was that which Matthew Arnold visioned as "the unplumbed, salt, estranging sea." The sea represents also the ungodly nations and rulers that rage against God and His people; and in this symbolic sense there could be no sea in the perfect world. Some of us love the sea. We were brought up near its waters and accustomed to the music of its waves. If there were no sea in the new world we should not like it there. But John was a Jew; and the sea never did appeal to the Jew. "The Jew never made a sailor." John, therefore, uses the sea as a symbol. It stood for separation, the estranging sea; and in the new world there will be no separation from God and from those whom we love. Some of us have the bodies of beloved dead resting in graves beyond the seas. We should like to stand and meditate beside those lonely graves in alien lands, but the "unplumbed, salt, estranging sea" comes in between: in heaven there will be no sea. The sea stands also for the mystery of life, it is *unplumbed,* with its dark unfathomed caves, but the time is coming when the sea shall give up its secrets. All our questions will be answered, all our problems solved, and all the mystery unveiled. The sea with its uncertain, restless, changing moods will be no more.

In that new world God dwells with men in the holy city. The saints look for a city which hath foundations, whose builder and maker is God, for "God ... hath prepared for them a city." (Heb. 11:16.) The Word of God Incarnate dwelt with men in the days of His flesh and they beheld something of His glory. In the new earth God makes His dwelling place with the redeemed. There is here no reference to a physical tab-

ernacle; for we are told later that in this holy city
there is no temple. (21:22.) "I will walk among you,
and will be your God, and ye shall be my people" was
the promise made to ancient Israel. (Lev. 26:12.)
Now that promise in all of its fullness is realized; and
the one people are enlarged into many "peoples." Sin
and death are destroyed, and so there will be no more
sorrow and crying. In the fellowship and companionship of this city of God, made ready as a bride adorned
for her husband, are to be found the entire company of
those who have washed their robes and made them
white in the blood of the Lamb, from the first man
who laid hold upon the promise of God in paradise
down to the last man, woman, or child who shall call
upon Christ in faith before the curtain of eternity shall
fall upon the stage of this world. As there is one God
and one Mediator between God and men, so also in the
ultimate issue there can be only one Church, one Bride
of Christ, in which all divisions of time and race and
class and creed are swept away. "We believe in one
holy catholic and apostolic church," chosen out of the
whole human race to everlasting life. "He that over-
cometh shall inherit these things; and I will be his God,
and he shall be my son." (21:7.)

In the verses that follow, 21:9—22:5, we have the
symbolic description of the Holy City. As we read this
description we should not imagine that we are in a jew-
eler's shop, or that we need the instruments of an ar-
chitect for the taking of measurements and the making
of calculations. John is carried in spirit to a great and
high mountain, from which he can gain a wide and
lofty view and see in the right perspective. From
thence he sees the holy city of Jerusalem coming down
out of heaven from God, having the glory of God. God
is her light; and the brightness of the divine presence
produces on John the effect of a dazzling brilliance, ra-
diating out from a great and luminous center, "like
unto a stone most precious, as it were a jasper stone,
clear as crystal." (21:11.) "The glory of God" was reflected on the face of Moses; the glory of the Lord

filled the tabernacle. Moses had prayed that he might see this glory unveiled, but he was denied that privilege, for no one could see it undimmed and live. This glory of God's manifest presence is the glory which John saw from his mount of vision. It is the full realization of Emmanuel, God with us.

The security of the city is symbolized by the wall, great and high, which surrounds it: it is a strong city, spacious, beautiful, and glorious. An easy entrance into it is provided by the twelve gates, three on each side. Twelve angels stand as guardians of the gates, but not to bar the way as in Eden; "He shall give his angels charge concerning thee." From every direction and every part of the world citizens may come and find an easy admission into the city. The measurement of the city was a guarantee of its preservation; and no significance is to be attached to the literal numbers of its dimensions. In form it was a perfect cube, expressive of symmetry and harmony. To the ancient mind the cube suggested perfection. The precious stones and gold of verses eighteen to twenty-one suggest the ideas of beauty and richness and splendor, and stand of course for spiritual realities. In the Holy City there is no temple (21:22), for none is needed: "The Lord God the Almighty, and the Lamb, are the temple thereof." The presence of God in all and through all makes it one vast sanctuary. The function of the earthly temple had been to symbolize the presence of God; but now we have a God-inhabited society, the perfected and eternal state of the Church in the manifest presence of God. The nations of the redeemed, the multitude which no man could number, shall walk in the light thereof; and the characteristics of all nations shall be harmonized into one in the perfected communion of the saints. Into this city shall be brought all that is true and beautiful and good; "the kings of the earth bring their glory into it." There is full and free access to God, for the gates are never shut. All evil and impurity are forever excluded. (21:25-27). Only those whose names are written in the Lamb's book of life may enter

in, leaving all their impurity and imperfection outside
that beautiful and sinless city.

In the final section of this vision (22:1-5) John
turns our thoughts from the wonderful structure of the
city to the blessedness of the life of its inhabitants. In
the book of Genesis we have Paradise Lost; and here
at the close of the Bible we have a picture of Paradise
Regained. The first paradise was the garden of Eden;
and here in the final paradise we have the picture of a
garden in a city. The heavenly world is pictured as a
city because redeemed humanity will constitute a community, a society, a Church. All that man lost—and
more—will be completely regained in the paradise
which John saw. In the beginning God's world was
good: "God saw every thing that he had made, and,
behold, it was very good." (Gen. 1:31.) But the world
which we know is no longer good. Its beauty is marred,
its glory is dimmed. Sin has entered the world, and
where sin is there is death. "The whole creation
groaneth and travaileth in pain." (Rom. 8:22.) John
shows us God's world as it shall be when His work of
redeeming and restoring grace in Christ is done: "Behold, I make all things new." (Rev. 21:5.) In this new
world there is life abundant, life everywhere, life eternal. This is symbolized by the river of water of life,
and by the tree of life, "bearing twelve manner of fruits,
yielding its fruit every month: and the leaves of the
tree were for the healing of the nations." (22:2.)
There is no sickness in the coming world, because by
the healing leaves of the tree of life all sickness has
been forever overcome. "There shall be no curse any
more." (22:3.) That pronounced on Adam in the first
paradise has been absolved and will never be renewed:
all the issues of the great primeval transgression are
done away.

The occupation of the citizens of the Holy City is
sketched in a final word: "His servants shall serve him
. . . and his name shall be on their foreheads. . . .
and they shall reign for ever and ever." (22:3-5.)
Service is the highest type and condition of life, either

here or hereafter; and the life of heaven will be a life of service. Heaven is not a silent place, but a place of song. It is not an idle place of placid repose, but a place of service.

We can sympathize with the longing for rest which finds expression in the epitaph of the woman who in this world had known only the weariness of work:

"Here lies a woman who always was tired,
   For she lived in a world where too much was re-
   quired.
   Weep not for me, friends, she said, for I'm going
   Where there'll neither be cooking nor washing nor
   sewing.

"I go where the loud hallelujahs are ringing,
   But I shall not take any part in the singing.
   Then weep not for me, friends, if death do us
   sever.
   For I'm going to do nothing for ever and ever."

But over against this we read that the saints in glory rest from their labors (14:13); and yet "they have no rest day and night" (4:8). Activity is the prelude to rest; and peace and companionship with God do not exclude activity. In the future world man's purified powers and capacities will be expressed in fuller service, free from all the laborious elements that make work in this world so often a thing of toil and pain. One of the chief joys of heaven will be the joy of loving service. In their service they shall see His face; and "his name shall be on their foreheads." To wear God's name is to bear a likeness to Him, to have "the imprint of His perfections." Those who serve God and see God will shine with His reflected glory. The name upon the forehead is also the symbol of possession, the sign of the divine ownership. Seeing God's face they shall know Him in all His fullness; serving Him, they shall shine with His glory.

We Christians need to think more of this promised

City of God. We are strangers and pilgrims in the earth. We have here no abiding home, but look for a city which hath the foundations, whose builder and maker is God. Charles M. Alexander some years ago told of a friend who went from the city into the country to recuperate from what he thought was a slight illness. He was far gone with tuberculosis, but, due to the deceptive nature of the disease, he thought that he was growing better day after day. One morning he said that he felt so much improved in health that he expected to return to the city on the following day. In the late afternoon his friend came to see him, and, much to his surprise, found him back in bed with a nurse in close attendance. "Why," he said, "I thought you were going to the city tomorrow!" The sick man's face lighted up, and he said: "I am going to a city, but it is a city where the living never die, and where no sickness and no sorrow can come." He died not many days later, and his friend, remembering his words, wrote these lines:

"I am going to a city
    Where the living never die,
    Where no sickness and no sorrow can molest;
From this body to release me
    Christ is speeding from on high;
    He will greet me and escort me to my rest."

And so the visions of John close. The remaining verses of chapter twenty-two are an epilogue to the main action of the book. The curtain upon the last act in the drama of the ages falls with the renewed promise of His coming, and with the acquiescent, longing cry of Christian faith: "Amen. Even so, come, Lord Jesus." (22:20.)[30] The whole book of Revelation circles around one central figure—the radiant figure of the Lamb of God which taketh away the sins of the world. At the very center of the new heaven and the new

[30] King James Version.

earth, in the midst of the Holy City, we see Jesus, all things now put under Him: "And the city hath no need of the sun, neither of the moon, to shine upon it: for the glory of God did lighten it, and the lamp thereof is the Lamb." (21:23.) And when we come down from the mount of vision to the plains of everyday life in the epilogue, we hear again the Lamb, "the tender Lamb, the blessed Lamb, the Lamb of Calvary": "I am the Alpha and the Omega, the first and the last, the beginning and the end." (22:13.)

In chapters four and five John's series of seven visions starts with a view of that calm and peace which reign eternal at the heart of the universe, before any disturbing storm or mystery of evil had yet appeared. In the following visions he carries us over and over again the troubled sea of the world's history. Each vision covers the whole period of history from the first coming of Christ down to the end of the age, when He comes again in power, glory, and judgment. In each vision there is the revelation of the same eternal principles of God's government, and the same assurance of the eventual triumph of the saints. The visions are not chronologically successive, but synchronous; and yet in each succeeding vision there is seen an ascending climax of judgments, moving steadily toward the final consummation. In the seventh and last vision we come back to the same level from which we started, the eternal peace of God. The tree of life is restored, and the saints shall reign for ever and ever. "The King of Evil is dead—long live the King of Love!" In this last vision, Christ the Redeemer and Prince of Peace is no longer potentially triumphant, but actually and forever victorious over all the enemies of God and man. Out of the darkness and welter of the storm-swept night of human history we come into the glorious dawn of a new and eternal day.

Dr. Clement Webb, in his book, *The Historical Element in Religion*,[31] says that "the historical element in

---

[31] Quotation used by permission of George Allen & Unwin, Ltd., publishers.

the Old Testament is not a mere collection of stories, but a history of the world, although no doubt a history of the world told from a special point of view and with a practical intent." The history is so related as to reveal the fact that the underlying principle which gives unity and meaning to the whole is God's government of the world, manifesting itself in different ways in different periods, but moving always toward the fulfillment of a divine purpose. It is only prophetic insight into the meaning of things and foresight of the coming Day of the Lord which enable one to see that the whole of history is divinely governed. This Day of the Lord to which the prophet pointed was "the consummation of the whole series of events" in human history. The author of Revelation, with true prophetic insight, sees that in the present the directing hand of God is often obscured by the power of evil. "The Most High ruleth in the kingdom of men." (Dan. 4:17.) "The kingdom is the Lord's; and he is the ruler over the nations." (Ps. 22:28.) In certain periods of trial and persecution, when the powers of evil seem regnant, His rule is veiled from the eyes of men. In the Day of the Lord the hidden meaning and divine purpose of history will come to light. In the end mankind shall see the glory of the Lord; and those who have faithfully followed Christ through all the varying experiences of life shall emerge victorious and enter in through the gates into the eternal city of God. John would have the distressed Christians of his generation share his prophetic insight into the meaning of things; and so, with a marvelous wealth of apocalyptic symbolism, he gives them a magnificent superview of history.

His book of Revelation begins with the power and glory of God. It carries us in parallel visions through the sin and sorrow, the death and darkness, of many intervening centuries; and brings us out at last into the radiance of the eternal morning of the new world: and there shall be no night there. The realization of the vision, "the riches of the glory of his inheritance in the saints," can only come with the coming of the King. And we have His promise: "Behold, I come quickly. Blessed is he that keepeth the words of the prophecy of this book."